Inspiratio

for the Most Memorable Wedding on Any Budget

For more inspirational ideas, visit
WeddingSolutions.com

Celebrating the Marriage of

Amy and Andrew

23 April 2005

La Venta Inn

Palos Verdes, California

Inspirational Ideas

for the Most Memorable Wedding on Any Budget

This beautiful photo guide is designed to inspire you in choosing the perfect look for your wedding. See everything from beautiful wedding attire and ceremony locations to elegant reception details and gifts. These gorgeous photographs will help you create the most memorable wedding on any budget!

For more inspirational ideas, visit WeddingSolutions.com

Planning the Most Memorable Wedding

ON ANY BUDGET

From America's Top Wedding Experts

Elizabeth & Alex Lluch

Authors of Over 30 Best-Selling Wedding Books

Wedding Solutions Publishing, Inc.

San Diego, California

Planning the Most
Memorable Wedding
ON ANY BUDGET

Written by Elizabeth & Alex Lluch
America's Top Wedding Experts

Published by Wedding Solutions Publishing, Inc.
San Diego, California 92119
© Copyright September 2006 by Wedding Solutions Publishing, Inc.

Floral Descriptions Written and Researched by:
Joan Hahn Perilla
Partner, Public Relations Marketing, Inc.
Marketing Consultant to the Flower Council of Holland

Design by:
Sarah Jang, Wedding Solutions Publishing, Inc.

Printed in China and Korea
ISBN-13: 978-1-887169-68-4
ISBN-10: 1-887169-68-7

CELEBRATING THE WEDDING OF

_____

AND

_____

TO BE MARRIED ON

_____

AT

_____

PHOTO CREDIT

A SPECIAL THANKS TO OUR CONTRIBUTING PHOTOGRAPHER

Karen French
Karen French Photography
8351 Elmcrest Lane
Huntington Beach, California 92646
(800) 734-6219
E-mail: info@karenfrenchphotography.com
Website: www.karenfrenchphotography.com
Available nationally and internationally - Based in Orange County, California

CONTENTS

CONTENTS

INTRODUCTION

CONGRATULATIONS ON YOUR ENGAGEMENT! You must be very excited to have found that special person with whom you will share the rest of your life. And you must be looking forward to what will be the happiest day of your life – your wedding! Planning a wedding can be fun and exciting, but it can also be very stressful; that is why Wedding Solutions created *Planning the Most Memorable Wedding on Any Budget.*

Planning the Most Memorable Wedding on Any Budget is a comprehensive guide that contains all the information you need to plan the wedding of your dreams. Whether you and your fiancé wish to celebrate with an intimate affair or a large scale production, the comprehensive Budget Analysis, Price Ranges, and Tips to Save Money provided in this book are sure to accommodate your budget.

This book focuses on a wedding planning checklist and budget worksheet that outlines the expenses that are typically incurred in a wedding and also provides a detailed explanation of each item. *Planning the Most Memorable Wedding on Any Budget* contains over 100 worksheets to keep you organized and on top of your plans. A twelve-month calendar allows you to record and keep track of important dates. In addition, we have added many other features that are a must for couples who want to easily and efficiently plan a successful wedding.

The book begins with a wedding planning checklist that lists everything you need to do or consider when planning your wedding and the best time frame in which to accomplish each activity. Many of the items in the checklist are preceded by the page number(s) where that item is explained within the book.

The checklist is followed by a comprehensive and detailed budget analysis, listing all the expenses that are typically incurred in a wedding as well as the percentage of the total budget that is typically spent in each category. Each expense item in the budget is preceded by the page number(s) where that item is explained within the book. This makes it very easy to find detailed information on each item.

The budget analysis is followed by a detailed description of each item in the budget including: Options, Things to Consider, Questions to Ask, Things To Beware Of, Tips to Save Money, and Price Ranges. Our clients find this format to be both informative and easy-to-use, and we know you will, too!

INTRODUCTION

Following the detailed description of each item in the budget are wedding timelines for your wedding party as well as your service providers. Use these timelines to keep everyone on schedule.

Next is a short chapter on wedding traditions that explains the symbolic meaning and historical purpose of some of the more common wedding traditions, as well as a list of "Do's and Don'ts" when planning your wedding.

We have also included a list of responsibilities for each member of your wedding party, in addition to the traditional formations for the ceremony, processional, and recessional for both Jewish and Christian weddings.

Other features include 20 pages of striking, full-color photographs to serve as a source of inspiration and ideas. A handy, portable, mini-planner containing your wedding planning checklist, budget analysis, wedding events at a glance, vendor contact information, calendar, and note pages allows you to keep all your important information with you at all times. The book's portable size, comprehensive information, and easy-to-read format will make it an essential wedding planner for couples with any wedding budget!

We are confident that you will enjoy planning your wedding with the help of *Planning the Most Memorable Wedding on Any Budget*. So come join the many couples who have used this book to plan a stress-free wedding. Also, if you know other Options, Things to Consider, Tips to Save Money, or anything else that you would like to see included in this book, please write to us at: Wedding Solutions; 7290 Navajo Road, Suite 207; San Diego, California 92119. We listen to brides and grooms like you – that is why *Planning the Most Memorable Wedding on Any Budget* has become one of the best wedding planners available today!

Sincerely,

Elizabeth H. Lluch

SWEET MEMORIES

THE MOMENT SOMEONE SPECIAL PROPOSES is a memory that is cherished forever. The story will be told over and over, to friends, family, children, and grandchildren...

How was your proposal special? Did he plan an elaborate scheme, or was it a simple, romantic display of his love for you? Did you propose to him? Every proposal is special and unique. You will have it forever, in your mind and in your heart.

Use the following pages to record that precious moment so the two of you can relive your memories together.

Answer the questions as you remember them. Let your words reflect the memory of each moment. Come back to these pages often as you plan your wedding. Reading about the day you got engaged will help to keep your romantic thoughts alive as you plan the event that will bind the two of you together for the rest of your lives!

THE PROPOSAL

Date: _____   Time: _____

Location: _____

He/she said/did: _____

_____

_____

_____

_____

_____

_____

_____

You said/did: _____

_____

_____

_____

_____

_____

_____

_____

Then we did/went to: _____

_____

_____

_____

_____

_____

My parents' reaction was:

His/her parents' reaction was:

My best friend's reaction was:

His/her best friend's reaction was:

NOTES

WEDDING EVENTS
AT A GLANCE

YOUR WEDDING WILL BE A CELEBRATION that will most likely span several different events. From the moment you get engaged to your last dance, your life will be filled with many special occasions.

Use the following worksheets to easily keep track of events, dates, locations, and contact information. Keeping these details in one place will help you plan ahead for each party and quickly reference important information.

Once you have finalized all of your events, make copies of these worksheets and distribute them to members of your wedding party, consultants, or vendors who would require this information.

WEDDING EVENTS AT A GLANCE

ENGAGEMENT PARTY DATE: _____

Engagement Party Time: _____

Engagement Party Location: _____

Contact Person: _____

Phone Number: _____

Website: _____

E-mail: _____

BRIDAL SHOWER DATE: _____

Bridal Shower Time: _____

Bridal Shower Location: _____

Contact Person: _____

Phone Number: _____

Website: _____

E-mail: _____

BACHELOR PARTY DATE: _____

Bachelor Party Time: _____

Bachelor Party Location: _____

Contact Person: _____

Phone Number: _____

Website: _____

E-mail: _____

BACHELORETTE PARTY DATE: _____

Bachelorette Party Time: _____

Bachelorette Party Location: _____

Contact Person: _____

Phone Number: _____

Website: _____

E-mail: _____

CEREMONY REHEARSAL DATE:

Ceremony Rehearsal Time:

Ceremony Rehearsal Location:

Contact Person:

Phone Number:

Website:

E-mail:

REHEARSAL DINNER DATE:

Rehearsal Dinner Time:

Rehearsal Dinner Location:

Contact Person:

Phone Number:

Website:

E-mail:

CEREMONY DATE:

Ceremony Time:

Ceremony Location:

Contact Person:

Phone Number:

Website:

E-mail:

RECEPTION DATE:

Reception Time:

Reception Location:

Contact Person:

Phone Number:

Website:

E-mail:

INFORMATION AT A GLANCE

VENDOR	Company	Contact	Phone #	Website/E-mail
Consultant				
Ceremony Site				
Reception Site				
Caterer				
Liquor Services				
Wedding Gown				
Tuxedo Rental				
Photographer				
Videographer				
Stationer				
Calligrapher				
Music: Ceremony				
Music: Reception				
Florist				
Bakery				
Decorations				
Ice Sculpture				
Party Favors				
Balloonist				
Transportation				
Rental & Supplies				
Gift Suppliers				
Valet Services				
Gift Attendant				
Rehearsal Dinner				

WEDDING PLANNING CHECKLIST

THE FOLLOWING WEDDING PLANNING CHECKLIST itemizes everything you need to do or consider when planning your wedding and the best time frame in which to accomplish each activity.

As you can see, many of the items are preceded by the page number(s) where they are explained in more detail within the book. This will quickly help you find the information you need.

This checklist assumes that you have at least nine months to plan your wedding. If your wedding is in less than nine months, just start at the beginning of the list and try to catch up as quickly as you can!

Use the boxes to the left of the items to check-off the activities as you accomplish them. This will enable you to see your progress and help you determine what has been done and what still needs to be done.

WEDDING PLANNING CHECKLIST

NINE MONTHS & EARLIER

PAGE

   ❑ Announce your engagement.

   ❑ Select a wedding date.

204 ❑ Hire a professional wedding consultant.

   ❑ Determine the type of wedding you want: location, formality, time of day, number of guests.

25-33 ❑ Determine budget and how expenses will be shared.

34   ❑ Develop a record-keeping system for payments made.

   ❑ Consolidate all guest lists: bride's, groom's, bride's family, groom's family, and organize those who:
    1) must be invited
    2) should be invited
    3) would be nice to invite

   ❑ Decide if you want to invite children.

35   ❑ Select and reserve the ceremony site.

35   ❑ Select and reserve the officiant.

NINE MONTHS & EARLIER (CONT'D)

PAGE

125 ❑ Select and reserve the reception site.

49-51 ❑ Select and order your bridal gown and headpiece.

   ❑ Determine color scheme.

67, 201 ❑ Send engagement notice with a photograph to your local newspaper.

14-15, 197-199, 247 ❑ Use the calendar provided to note all important activities: showers, luncheons, parties, get-togethers, etc.

   ❑ If ceremony or reception is at home, arrange for home or garden improvements as needed.

63   ❑ Select and book the photographer.

   ❑ Order passport, visa, or birth certificate if needed for your honeymoon or marriage license.

232-233 ❑ Select maid of honor, best man, bridesmaids and ushers (approx. one usher per 50 guests).

WEDDING PLANNING CHECKLIST

SIX TO NINE MONTHS BEFORE WEDDING

PAGE

235 ❑ Select flower girl and ring bearer.

❑ Give the *Wedding Party Responsibility Cards* to your wedding party. These cards are published by Wedding Solutions and are available at major book stores.

❑ Reserve your wedding night bridal suite.

61 ❑ Select attendants' dresses, shoes, and accessories.

126 ❑ Select and book your caterer, if needed.

147 ❑ Select and book ceremony musicians.

148 ❑ Select and book reception musicians or DJ.

60-62 ❑ Schedule fittings and delivery dates for yourself, attendants, flower girl, and ring bearer.

77 ❑ Select and book videographer.

161 ❑ Select and book florist.

FOUR TO SIX MONTHS BEFORE WEDDING

PAGE

195 ❑ Start shopping for each other's wedding gifts.

185 ❑ Reserve rental items needed for ceremony.

102 ❑ Finalize guest list.

83-93 ❑ Select and order wedding invitations, announcements, and other stationery such as thank-you notes, wedding programs, and seating cards.

93, 102, 123 ❑ Address invitations or hire a calligrapher.

15, 199 ❑ Set date, time, and location for the rehearsal dinner.

118 ❑ Arrange accommodations for out-of-town guests.

❑ Start planning your honeymoon.

133 ❑ Select and book all miscellaneous services, i.e. gift attendant, valet parking, babysitting, etc.

❑ Register for gifts.

52-53 ❑ Buy shoes and accessories.

53 ❑ Break in your shoes.

WEDDING PLANNING CHECKLIST

TWO TO FOUR MONTHS BEFORE WEDDING

PAGE

155 ❏ Select bakery and order wedding cake.

131, ❏ Order party favors.
143

179 ❏ Select and order room decorations.

    ❏ Purchase honeymoon attire and luggage.

181 ❏ Select and book transportation for wedding day.

201 ❏ Check blood test and marriage license requirements.

    ❏ Shop for wedding rings and have them engraved.

    ❏ Consider having your teeth cleaned or bleached.

202 ❏ Consider writing a will and/or prenuptial agreement.

    ❏ Plan activities for out-of-town guests both before and after the wedding.

195- ❏ Purchase gifts for wedding
196   attendants.

SIX TO EIGHT WEEKS BEFORE WEDDING

PAGE

83-91, ❏ Mail invitations. Include
102   accommodation choices and a map to assist guests in finding the ceremony and reception sites.

92, ❏ Maintain a record of RSVPs
102   and all gifts received. Send thank-you notes upon receipt of gifts.

53-54 ❏ Determine hair style and makeup.

53-54 ❏ Schedule to have your hair, makeup and nails done the day of the wedding.

36-37 ❏ Finalize shopping for
157   wedding day accessories, such as guest book, ring pillow, toasting glasses, etc.

    ❏ Set up an area or a table in your home to display gifts as you receive them.

201 ❏ Check with your local newspapers for wedding announcement requirements.

67 ❏ Have your formal wedding portrait taken.

201 ❏ Send announcement and photograph to your local newspapers.

SIX TO EIGHT WEEKS BEFORE WEDDING (CONT'D)

PAGE

209-211 ❑ Change name and address on driver's license, social security card, insurance policies, bank accounts, etc.

54-56 62 ❑ Select and reserve wedding attire for groom, ushers, father of the bride, and ring bearer.

36 ❑ Select a guest book attendant. Decide where and when to have guests sign in.

❑ Mail invitations to rehearsal dinner.

201 ❑ Get blood test and health certificate.

201 ❑ Obtain marriage license.

198 ❑ Plan a luncheon or dinner with your bridesmaids. Give them their gifts at that time or at the rehearsal dinner.

223 ❑ Find "something old, something new, something borrowed, something blue, and a six pence (or shiny penny) for your shoe."

126-130, 142, 146 ❑ Finalize your menu, beverage and alcohol order.

TWO TO SIX WEEKS BEFORE WEDDING

PAGE

❑ Confirm ceremony details with your officiant.

61 ❑ Arrange final fitting of bridesmaids' dresses.

60 ❑ Have final fitting of your gown and head piece.

90, 199 ❑ Finalize rehearsal dinner plans; arrange seating and write names on place cards.

161, 174-176 ❑ Make final floral selections.

214-217 ❑ Make a detailed timeline for your wedding party.

218-221 ❑ Make a detailed timeline for your service providers.

218-221 ❑ Confirm details with all service providers, including attire. Give them a copy of your wedding timeline.

❑ Start packing for your honeymoon.

92, 114 ❑ Finalize addressing and stamping announcements.

122, 244 ❑ Decide when and where to form a receiving line, if desired.

TWO TO SIX WEEKS BEFORE WEDDING (CONT'D)

PAGE

    ❑ Contact guests who haven't yet responded.

    ❑ Pick up rings and check for fit.

74-76 ❑ Meet with photographer and confirm special photos you want taken.

77 ❑ Meet with videographer and confirm special events or people you want videotaped.

42,   ❑ Meet with musicians and
147-   confirm music to be played
154   during special events such as the first dance.

92,   ❑ Continue writing thank-you
102   notes as gifts arrive.

61-   ❑ Remind bridesmaids and
62   ushers of when and where to pick up their wedding attire.

54 ❑ Purchase the lipstick, nail polish, and other accessories for your bridesmaids.

44-45 ❑ Determine ceremony seating for special guests. Give a list to the ushers.

90,   ❑ Plan reception layout and
140-   seating with your site
141   manager or caterer. Write names on place cards for arranged seating.

THE LAST WEEK

PAGE

60-62 ❑ Pick up wedding attire and make sure everything fits.

    ❑ Do final guest count and notify your caterer or reception site manager.

245- ❑ Gather everything you will
246   need for the rehearsal and wedding day.

232 ❑ Arrange for someone to drive the getaway car.

218- ❑ Review the schedule of
221   events and last minute arrangements with your service providers. Give them each a detailed timeline.

    ❑ Confirm all honeymoon reservations and accommodations. Pick up tickets and travelers checks.

    ❑ Finish packing your suitcases for the honeymoon.

102 ❑ Familiarize yourself with guests' names. It will help during the receiving line and reception.

    ❑ Notify the Post Office to hold your mail while you are away on your honeymoon.

WEDDING PLANNING CHECKLIST

THE REHEARSAL DAY

PAGE

245 ❑ Review list of things to bring to the rehearsal.

❑ Put suitcases in getaway car.

❑ Give your bridesmaids the accessories you want them to wear for the wedding.

232 ❑ Give best man the officiant's fee and any other checks for service providers. Instruct him to deliver these checks the day of the wedding.

❑ Arrange for someone to bring accessories; flower basket, ring pillow, guest book and pen, napkins, etc. to the ceremony and reception.

92, ❑ Arrange for someone to mail
232 announcements the day after the wedding.

185, ❑ Arrange for someone to
232 return rental items such as tuxedos, slip, and cake pillars after the wedding.

214- ❑ Provide each member of
217 your wedding party with a detailed schedule of events/ timeline for the wedding.

44-45 ❑ Review ceremony seating
233 with ushers.

THE WEDDING DAY

PAGE

246 ❑ Review list of things to bring to the ceremony.

❑ Give the groom's ring to the maid of honor.

❑ Give the bride's ring to the best man.

214- ❑ Simply follow your detailed
217 schedule of events.

❑ Relax and enjoy your wedding!

NOTES

BUDGET ANALYSIS

THIS COMPREHENSIVE BUDGET ANALYSIS has been designed to provide you with all the expenses that can be incurred in any size wedding, including such hidden costs as taxes, gratuities, postage, and other "items" that can easily add up to thousands of dollars in a wedding. After you have completed this budget, you will have a much better idea of what your wedding will cost. You can then prioritize and allocate your expenses accordingly.

This budget is divided into fifteen categories: Ceremony, Wedding Attire, Photography, Videography, Stationery, Reception, Music, Bakery, Flowers, Decorations, Transportation, Rental Items, Gifts, Parties, and Miscellaneous.

At the beginning of each category is the percentage of your total wedding budget that is typically spent in that category, based on national averages. Multiply your intended wedding budget by this percentage and write that amount in the "Typically" space provided.

To determine the total cost of your wedding, estimate the amount of money you will spend on each item in the budget analysis and write that amount in the "Budget" column after each item. Next to each expense item is the page number where you can find detailed information about it. Items printed in italics are traditionally paid for by the groom or his family.

Add all the "Budget" amounts within each category and write the total amount in the "Subtotal" space at the end of each category. Then add all the "Subtotal" figures to come up with your final wedding budget. The "Actual" column is for you to input your actual expenses as you purchase items or hire your service providers. Writing down the actual expenses will help you stay within your budget.

For example, if your total wedding budget is $60,000, write this amount at the top of page 28. To figure your typical ceremony expenses, multiply $60,000 x .05 (5%) = $3,000.00. Write this amount on the "Typically" line in the "Ceremony" category to serve as a guide for all your ceremony expenses.

If you find after adding up all your "Subtotals" that the total amount is more than what you had in mind to spend, simply decide which items are more important to you and adjust your expenses accordingly.

CHECKLIST OF BUDGET ITEMS

CEREMONY

- ❑ Ceremony Site Fee
- ❑ *Officiant's Fee*
- ❑ *Officiant's Gratuity*
- ❑ Guest Book/Pen/Penholder
- ❑ Ring Bearer Pillow
- ❑ Flower Girl Basket

WEDDING ATTIRE

- ❑ Bridal Gown
- ❑ Alterations
- ❑ Headpiece/Veil
- ❑ Gloves
- ❑ Jewelry
- ❑ Garter/Stockings
- ❑ Shoes
- ❑ Hairdresser
- ❑ Makeup Artist
- ❑ Manicure/Pedicure
- ❑ *Groom's Formal Wear*

PHOTOGRAPHY

- ❑ Bride & Groom's Album
- ❑ Parents' Album
- ❑ Extra Prints
- ❑ Proofs/Previews
- ❑ Negatives/Digital Files
- ❑ Engagement Photograph
- ❑ Formal Bridal Portrait

VIDEOGRAPHY

- ❑ Main Video
- ❑ Titles
- ❑ Extra Hours
- ❑ Photo Montage
- ❑ Extra Copies

STATIONERY

- ❑ Invitations
- ❑ Response Cards
- ❑ Reception Cards
- ❑ Ceremony Cards
- ❑ Pew Cards
- ❑ Seating/Place Cards
- ❑ Rain Cards
- ❑ Maps
- ❑ Ceremony Programs
- ❑ Announcements
- ❑ Thank-You Notes
- ❑ Stamps
- ❑ Calligraphy
- ❑ Napkins/Matchbooks

RECEPTION

- ❑ Reception Site Fee
- ❑ Hors D' Oeuvres
- ❑ Main Meal/Caterer
- ❑ Liquor/Beverages
- ❑ Bartending/Bar Set-up Fee
- ❑ Corkage Fee

RECEPTION (CONT'D)

- ❑ Fee to Pour Coffee
- ❑ Service Providers' Meals
- ❑ Gratuity
- ❑ Party Favors
- ❑ Disposable Cameras
- ❑ Rose Petals/Rice
- ❑ Gift Attendant
- ❑ Parking Fee/Valet Services

MUSIC

- ❑ Ceremony Music
- ❑ Reception Music

BAKERY

- ❑ Wedding Cake
- ❑ *Groom's Cake*
- ❑ Cake Delivery/Set-Up Fee
- ❑ Cake-Cutting Fee
- ❑ Cake Top
- ❑ Cake Knife/Toasting Glasses

FLOWERS

BOUQUETS

- ❑ *Bride*
- ❑ Tossing
- ❑ Maid of Honor
- ❑ Bridesmaids

Items in italics are traditionally paid for by the groom or his family.

CHECKLIST OF BUDGET ITEMS

FLOWERS (CONT'D)

FLORAL HAIRPIECES
- ❑ Maid of Honor/ Bridesmaids
- ❑ Flower Girl

CORSAGES
- ❑ *Bride's Going Away*
- ❑ *Family Members*

BOUTONNIERES
- ❑ *Groom*
- ❑ *Ushers/Other Family Members*

CEREMONY
- ❑ Main Altar
- ❑ Altar Candelabra
- ❑ Aisle Pews

RECEPTION SITE
- ❑ Reception Site
- ❑ Head Table
- ❑ Guest Tables
- ❑ Buffet Table
- ❑ Punch Table
- ❑ Cake Table
- ❑ Cake
- ❑ Cake Knife
- ❑ Toasting Glasses
- ❑ Floral Delivery/Set-up

DECORATIONS
- ❑ Table Centerpieces
- ❑ Balloons

TRANSPORTATION
- ❑ Transportation

RENTAL ITEMS
- ❑ Bridal Slip
- ❑ Ceremony Accessories
- ❑ Tent/Canopy
- ❑ Dance Floor
- ❑ Tables/Chairs
- ❑ Linen/Tableware
- ❑ Heaters
- ❑ Lanterns
- ❑ Other

GIFTS
- ❑ *Bride's Gift*
- ❑ Groom's Gift
- ❑ Bridesmaids' Gifts
- ❑ *Ushers' Gifts*

PARTIES
- ❑ Bridesmaids' Luncheon
- ❑ *Rehearsal Dinner*

MISCELLANEOUS
- ❑ Newspaper Announcement
- ❑ *Marriage License*
- ❑ *Prenuptial Agreement*
- ❑ Bridal Gown Preservation
- ❑ Bridal Bouquet Preservation

- ❑ Wedding Consultant
- ❑ Wedding Planning Online
- ❑ Taxes

Items in italics are traditionally paid for by the groom or his family.

BUDGET ANALYSIS

WEDDING BUDGET	Budget	Actual
YOUR TOTAL WEDDING BUDGET	$	$
CEREMONY (Typically = 5% of Budget)	$	$
pg. 35 Ceremony Site Fee	$	$
pg. 35 *Officiant's Fee*	$	$
pg. 36 *Officiant's Gratuity*	$	$
pg. 36 Guest Book/Pen/Penholder	$	$
pg. 37 Ring Bearer Pillow	$	$
pg. 37 Flower Girl Basket	$	$
SUBTOTAL 1	$	$
WEDDING ATTIRE (Typically = 10% of Budget)	$	$
pg. 49 Bridal Gown	$	$
pg. 51 Alterations	$	$
pg. 51 Headpiece/Veil	$	$
pg. 52 Gloves	$	$
pg. 52 Jewelry	$	$
pg. 53 Garter/Stockings	$	$
pg. 53 Shoes	$	$
pg. 53 Hairdresser	$	$
pg. 54 Makeup Artist	$	$
pg. 54 Manicure/Pedicure	$	$
pg. 55 *Groom's Formal Wear*	$	$
SUBTOTAL 2	$	$
PHOTOGRAPHY (Typically = 9% of Budget)	$	$
pg. 63 Bride & Groom's Album	$	$
pg. 65 Parents' Album	$	$
pg. 65 Extra Prints	$	$
pg. 65 Proofs/Previews	$	$

Items in italics are traditionally paid for by the groom or his family.

	Budget	Actual
pg. 66 Negatives/Digital Files	$	$
pg. 67 Engagement Photograph	$	$
pg. 67 Formal Bridal Portrait	$	$
SUBTOTAL 3	$	$
VIDEOGRAPHY (Typically = 5% of Budget)	$	$
pg. 77 Main Video	$	$
pg. 78 Titles	$	$
pg. 78 Extra Hours	$	$
pg. 78 Photo Montage	$	$
pg. 79 Extra Copies	$	$
SUBTOTAL 4	$	$
STATIONERY (Typically = 4% of Budget)	$	$
pg. 83 Invitations	$	$
pg. 88 Response Cards	$	$
pg. 88 Reception Cards	$	$
pg. 89 Ceremony Cards	$	$
pg. 90 Pew Cards	$	$
pg. 90 Seating/Place Cards	$	$
pg. 91 Rain Cards	$	$
pg. 91 Maps	$	$
pg. 91 Ceremony Programs	$	$
pg. 92 Announcements	$	$
pg. 92 Thank-You Notes	$	$
pg. 92 Stamps	$	$
pg. 93 Calligraphy	$	$
pg. 93 Napkins/Matchbooks	$	$
SUBTOTAL 5	$	$

Items in italics are traditionally paid for by the groom or his family.

BUDGET ANALYSIS

	Budget	Actual
RECEPTION (Typically = 35% of Budget)	$	$
pg. 125 Reception Site Fee	$	$
pg. 126 Hors D' Oeuvres	$	$
pg. 126 Main Meal/Caterer	$	$
pg. 128 Liquor/Beverages	$	$
pg. 129 Bartending/Bar Set-Up Fee	$	$
pg. 130 Corkage Fee	$	$
pg. 130 Fee To Pour Coffee	$	$
pg. 130 Service Providers' Meals	$	$
pg. 131 Gratuity	$	$
pg. 131 Party Favors	$	$
pg. 131 Disposable Cameras	$	$
pg. 132 Rose Petals/Rice	$	$
pg. 133 Gift Attendant	$	$
pg. 133 Parking Fee/Valet Services	$	$
SUBTOTAL 6	$	$
MUSIC (Typically = 5% of Budget)	$	$
pg. 147 Ceremony Music	$	$
pg. 148 Reception Music	$	$
SUBTOTAL 7	$	$
BAKERY (Typically = 2% of Budget)	$	$
pg. 155 Wedding Cake	$	$
pg. 156 *Groom's Cake*	$	$
pg. 156 Cake Delivery/Set-up Fee	$	$
pg. 156 Cake-Cutting Fee	$	$
pg. 157 Cake Top	$	$
pg. 157 Cake Knife/Toasting Glasses	$	$
SUBTOTAL 8	$	$

Items in italics are traditionally paid for by the groom or his family.

	Budget	Actual
FLOWERS (Typically = 6% of Budget)	$	$
BOUQUETS		
pg. 161 *Bride*	$	$
pg. 162 Tossing	$	$
pg. 163 Maid of Honor	$	$
pg. 163 Bridesmaids	$	$
FLORAL HAIRPIECES		
pg. 164 Maid of Honor/Bridesmaids	$	$
pg. 164 Flower Girl	$	$
CORSAGES		
pg. 164 *Bride's Going Away*	$	$
pg. 165 *Family Members*	$	$
BOUTONNIERES		
pg. 165 *Groom*	$	$
pg. 166 *Ushers and Other Family Members*	$	$
CEREMONY SITE FLOWERS		
pg. 166 Main Altar	$	$
pg. 167 Altar Candelabra	$	$
pg. 167 Aisle Pews	$	$
RECEPTION SITE FLOWERS		
pg. 168 Reception Site	$	$
pg. 168 Head Table	$	$
pg. 169 Guest Tables	$	$
pg. 169 Buffet Table	$	$
pg. 170 Punch Table	$	$
pg. 170 Cake Table	$	$
pg. 170 Cake	$	$
pg. 170 Cake Knife	$	$
pg. 171 Toasting Glasses	$	$

Items in italics are traditionally paid for by the groom or his family.

BUDGET ANALYSIS

	Budget	Actual
pg. 171 Floral Delivery/Set-up	$	$
SUBTOTAL 9	$	$
DECORATIONS (Typically = 3% of Budget)	$	$
pg. 179 Table Centerpieces	$	$
pg. 179 Balloons	$	$
SUBTOTAL 10	$	$
TRANSPORTATION (Typically = 2% of Budget)	$	$
pg. 181 Transportation	$	$
SUBTOTAL 11	$	$
RENTAL ITEMS (Typically = 3% of Budget)	$	$
pg. 185 Bridal Slip	$	$
pg. 185 Ceremony Accessories	$	$
pg. 186 Tent/Canopy	$	$
pg. 187 Dance Floor	$	$
pg. 187 Tables/Chairs	$	$
pg. 187 Linen/Tableware	$	$
pg. 188 Heaters	$	$
pg. 188 Lanterns	$	$
pg. 188 Other Rental Items	$	$
SUBTOTAL 12	$	$
GIFTS (Typically = 3% of Budget)	$	$
pg. 195 *Bride's Gift*	$	$
pg. 195 Groom's Gift	$	$
pg. 195 Bridesmaids' Gifts	$	$
pg. 196 *Ushers' Gifts*	$	$
SUBTOTAL 13	$	$

Items in italics are traditionally paid for by the groom or his family.

	Budget	Actual
PARTIES (Typically = 4% of Budget)	$	$
pg. 198 Bridesmaids' Luncheon	$	$
pg. 199 *Rehearsal Dinner*	$	$
SUBTOTAL 14	$	$
MISCELLANEOUS (Typically = 4% of Budget)	$	$
pg. 201 Newspaper Announcements	$	$
pg. 201 *Marriage License*	$	$
pg. 202 *Prenuptial Agreement*	$	$
pg. 203 Bridal Gown Preservation	$	$
pg. 203 Bridal Bouquet Preservation	$	$
pg. 204 Wedding Consultant	$	$
pg. 205 Wedding Planning Online	$	$
pg. 205 Taxes	$	$
SUBTOTAL 15	$	$

GRAND TOTAL

	Budget	Actual
(Add "Budget" & "Actual" Subtotals 1-15)	$	$

Items in italics are traditionally paid for by the groom or his family.

VENDOR PAYMENT TRACKING CHART

VENDOR	Business Name & Phone #	Website & E-mail	Contract Date & Total Cost	Deposit & Date	Final Pay. & Date
Consultant					
Ceremony Site					
Officiant					
Reception Site					
Caterer					
Liquor Services					
Wedding Gown					
Tuxedo Rental					
Photographer					
Videographer					
Stationer					
Calligrapher					
Music: Ceremony					
Music: Reception					
Florist					
Bakery					
Decorations					
Ice Sculpture					
Party Favors					
Balloonist					
Transportation					
Rental & Supplies					
Gift Suppliers					
Valet Services					
Gift Attendant					
Rehearsal Dinner					

CEREMONY

YOUR CEREMONY IS A REFLECTION OF WHO YOU ARE. It can be as simple or as elaborate as you desire. Many people choose to have a traditional ceremony in a church, while others have taken their special day outdoors to a park or to the beach. These days, anything goes!

CEREMONY SITE FEE

The ceremony site fee is the fee to rent a facility for your wedding. In churches, cathedrals, chapels, temples, or synagogues, this fee may include the organist, wedding coordinator, custodian, changing rooms for the bridal party, and miscellaneous items such as kneeling cushions, aisle runner, and candelabra. Be sure to ask what the site fee includes prior to booking a facility. Throughout this book, the word "church" will be used to refer to the site where the ceremony will take place.

Options: Churches, temples, cathedrals, chapels, synagogues, private-homes, gardens, hotels and resorts, clubs, halls, parks, museums, yachts, wineries, beaches, and more.

Things to Consider: Your selection of a ceremony site will be influenced by the formality of your wedding, the season of the year, the number of guests expected, and your religious affiliation.

Make sure you ask about restrictions or guidelines regarding photography, videography, music, decorations, candles, and rice or rose petal-tossing.

Consider issues such as proximity of the ceremony site to the reception site, parking availability, handicapped accessibility, and time constraints.

Tips to Save Money: Have your ceremony at the same facility as your reception to save a second rental fee. Set a realistic guest list and stick to it. Hire an experienced wedding consultant. At a church or temple, ask if there is another wedding that day and share the cost of floral decorations with that bride. Membership in a church, temple or club can reduce rental fees. At a garden wedding, have guests stand and omit the cost of renting chairs.

Price Range: $100 - $1,000

OFFICIANT'S FEE

The officiant's fee is the fee paid to the person who performs your wedding ceremony.

Options: Priest, Clergyman, Minister, Pastor, Chaplain, Rabbi, Judge, or Justice of the Peace. Discuss with your officiant the readings you would like incorporated into your ceremony.

Some popular readings are:

Beatitudes	Corinthians 13:1-13	Ecclesiastes 3:1-9
Ephesians 3:14-19; 5:1-2	Genesis 1:26-28	Genesis 2:4-9, 15-24
Hosea 2:19-21	Isaiah 61:10I	John 4:7-16
John 15:9-12, 17:22-24	Mark 10:6-9	Proverbs 31:10-31
Romans 12:1-2, 9-18	Ruth 1:16-17	Tobit 8:56-58

Things to Consider: Some officiants may not accept a fee, depending on your relationship with him/her. If a fee is refused, send a donation to the officiant's church or synagogue.

Price Range: $100 - $500

OFFICIANT'S GRATUITY

The officiant's gratuity is a discretionary amount of money given to the officiant.

Things to Consider: This amount should depend on your relationship with the officiant and the amount of time s/he has spent with you prior to the ceremony. The groom puts this fee in a sealed envelope and gives it to his best man or wedding consultant, who gives it to the officiant either before or immediately after the ceremony.

Price Range: $50 - $250

GUEST BOOK/PEN/PENHOLDER

The guest book is a formal register that your guests sign as they arrive at the ceremony or reception. It serves as a memento of who attended your wedding. This book is often placed outside the ceremony or reception site, along with an elegant pen and penholder. A guest book attendant is responsible for inviting all guests to sign-in. A younger sibling or close friend who is not part of the wedding party may be well-suited for this position.

Options: There are many styles of guest books, pens, and penholders to choose from. Some books have space for your guests to write a short note to the bride and groom.

Things to Consider: Make sure you have more than one pen in case one runs out of ink. If you are planning a large ceremony (over 300 guests), consider having more than one book and pen so that your guests don't have to wait in line to sign-in.

Price Range: $30 - $100

RING BEARER PILLOW

The ring bearer, usually a boy between the ages of four and eight, carries the bride and groom's rings or mock rings on a pillow. He follows the maid of honor and precedes the flower girl or bride in the processional.

Options: These pillows come in many styles and colors. You can find them at most gift shops, bridal boutiques and online stores that sell wedding accessories.

Things to Consider: If the ring bearer is very young (less than seven years), place mock rings on the pillow in place of the real rings to prevent losing them. If mock rings are used, instruct your ring bearer to put the pillow upside down during the recessional so your guests don't see them.

Tips to Save Money: Make your own ring bearer pillow by taking a small white pillow and attaching a pretty ribbon to it to hold the rings.

Price Range: $15 - $75

FLOWER GIRL BASKET

The flower girl, usually between the ages of four and eight, carries a basket filled with flowers, rose, or paper rose petals to strew as she walks down the aisle. She follows the ring bearer or maid of honor and precedes the bride during the processional.

Options: Flower girl baskets come in many styles and colors. You can find them at most florists, gift shops, bridal boutiques, and online stores that sell wedding accessories.

Things to Consider: Discuss any restrictions regarding rose petal, flower, or paper-tossing with your ceremony site. Select a basket which complements your guest book and ring bearer pillow. If the flower girl is very young (less than seven years), consider giving her a small bouquet instead of a flower basket.

Tips to Save Money: Ask your florist if you can borrow a basket and attach a pretty white bow to it.

Price Range: $20 - $75

CEREMONY SITE COMPARISON CHART

QUESTIONS	POSSIBILITY 1
What is the name of the ceremony site?	
What is the website and e-mail of the ceremony site?	
What is the address of the ceremony site?	
What is the name and phone number of my contact person?	
What dates and times are available?	
Do vows need to be approved?	
What is the ceremony site fee?	
What is the payment policy?	
What is the cancellation policy?	
Does the facility have liability insurance?	
What are the minimum and maximum number of guests allowed?	
What is the denomination, if any, of the facility?	
What restrictions are there with regards to religion?	
Is an officiant available? At what cost?	
Are outside officiants allowed?	
Are any musical instruments available for our use?	
If so, what is the fee?	

CEREMONY SITE COMPARISON CHART

POSSIBILITY 2	POSSIBILITY 3

CEREMONY SITE COMPARISON CHART

QUESTIONS	POSSIBILITY 1
What music restrictions are there, if any?	
What photography restrictions are there, if any?	
What videography restrictions are there, if any?	
Are there are any restrictions for rice/petal-tossing?	
Are candlelight ceremonies allowed?	
What floral decorations are available/allowed?	
When is my rehearsal to be scheduled?	
Is there handicap accessibility and parking?	
How many parking spaces are available for my wedding party?	
Where are they located?	
How many parking spaces are available for my guests?	
What rental items are necessary?	
What is the fee?	
Other:	
Other:	
Other:	
Other:	

CEREMONY SITE COMPARISON CHART

POSSIBILITY 2	POSSIBILITY 3

READING & MUSIC SELECTIONS

Source	Selection	Read By	When

When	Selection	Composer	Played By
Prelude 1			
Prelude 2			
Processional			
Bride's Processional			
Ceremony 1			
Ceremony 2			
Recessional			
Postlude			

BRIDE'S VOWS

GROOM'S VOWS

PERSONALIZED RING CEREMONY

PEW SEATING ARRANGEMENTS

Complete this form only after finalizing your guest list.

BRIDE'S FAMILY SECTION

• **PEW** __

_____
_____
_____
_____
_____
_____

• **PEW** __

_____
_____
_____
_____
_____
_____

• **PEW** __

_____
_____
_____
_____
_____
_____

• **PEW** __

_____
_____
_____
_____
_____
_____

• **PEW** __

_____
_____
_____
_____
_____
_____

• **PEW** __

_____
_____
_____
_____
_____
_____

• **PEW** __

_____
_____
_____
_____
_____
_____

• **PEW** __

_____
_____
_____
_____
_____
_____

PEW SEATING ARRANGEMENTS

Complete this form only after finalizing your guest list.

GROOM'S FAMILY SECTION

• PEW __

_____
_____
_____
_____
_____
_____
_____

• PEW __

_____
_____
_____
_____
_____
_____
_____

• PEW __

_____
_____
_____
_____
_____
_____
_____

• PEW __

_____
_____
_____
_____
_____
_____
_____

• PEW __

_____
_____
_____
_____
_____
_____
_____

• PEW __

_____
_____
_____
_____
_____
_____
_____

• PEW __

_____
_____
_____
_____
_____
_____
_____

• PEW __

_____
_____
_____
_____
_____
_____
_____

NOTES

UNIQUE
WEDDING IDEAS

IDEAS TO PERSONALIZE YOUR CEREMONY

Regardless of your religious affiliation, there are numerous ways in which you can personalize your wedding ceremony to add a more creative touch. If you're planning a religious ceremony at a church or temple, be sure to discuss all ideas with your officiant.

The following list incorporates some ideas to personalize your wedding ceremony:

- Invite the bride's mother to be part of the processional. Have her walk down the aisle with you and your father (this is the traditional Jewish processional.)
- Invite the groom's parents to be part of the processional also.
- Ask friends and family members to perform special readings.
- Ask a friend or family member with musical talent to perform at the ceremony.
- Incorporate poetry and/or literature into your readings.
- Change places with the officiant and face your guests during the ceremony.
- Light a unity candle to symbolize your two lives joining together as one.
- Drink wine from a shared "loving" cup to symbolize bonding with each other.
- Hand a rose to each of your mothers as you pass by them during the recessional.
- Release white doves into the air after being pronounced "husband and wife."
- If the ceremony is held outside on a grassy area, have your guests toss grass or flower seeds over you instead of rice.
- Publicly express gratitude for all that your parents have done for you.
- Use a canopy to designate an altar for a non-church setting. Decorate it in ways that are symbolic or meaningful to you.
- Burn incense to give the ceremony an exotic feeling.

UNIQUE WEDDING IDEAS

IDEAS TO PERSONALIZE YOUR MARRIAGE VOWS

Regardless of your religious affiliation and whether you're planning a church or outdoor ceremony, there are ways in which you can personalize your marriage vows to make them more meaningful for you. As with all your ceremony plans, be sure to discuss your ideas for marriage vows with your officiant.

The following are some ideas that you might want to consider when planning your marriage vows:

- You and your fiancé could write your own personal marriage vows and keep them secret from one another until the actual ceremony.

- Incorporate your guests and family members into your vows by acknowledging their presence at the ceremony.

- Describe what you cherish most about your partner and what you hope for your future together.

- Describe your commitment to and love for one another.

- Discuss your feelings and beliefs about marriage.

- If either of you has children from a previous marriage, mention these children in your vows and discuss your mutual love for and commitment to them.

ATTIRE

BRIDAL GOWNS COME IN A VARIETY OF STYLES, materials, colors, lengths, and prices. You should order your gown at least four to six months before your wedding if your gown has to be made to order, fitted, or altered.

BRIDAL GOWN

Options: Different gown styles can help create a shorter, taller, heavier, or thinner look. Here are some tips:

• **A short, heavy figure:** To look taller and slimmer, avoid knit fabrics. Use the princess or A-line style. Chiffon is the best fabric choice because it produces a floating effect and camouflages weight.

• **A short, thin figure:** A shirtwaist or natural waist style with bouffant skirt will produce a taller, more rounded figure. Chiffon, velvet, lace, and Schiffli net are probably the best fabric choices.

• **A tall, heavy figure:** Princess or A-line are the best styles for slimming the figure; satin, chiffon and lace fabrics are recommended.

• **A tall, thin figure:** Tiers or flounces will help reduce the impression of height. A shirtwaist or natural waist style with a full skirt are ideal choices. Silk, satin, and lace are the best fabrics.

The guidelines below will help you select the most appropriate gown for your wedding:

Informal wedding:
> Street-length gown or suit
> Corsage or small bouquet
> No veil or train

Semi-formal wedding:
> Floor-length gown
> Chapel train
> Finger-tip veil
> Small bouquet

ATTIRE

Formal daytime wedding:
> Floor-length gown
> Chapel or sweep train
> Fingertip veil or hat
> Gloves
> Medium-sized bouquet

Formal evening wedding:
> Same as formal daytime
> except longer veil

Very formal wedding:
> Floor-length gown
> Cathedral train
> Full-length veil
> Elaborate headpiece
> Long sleeves or long arm covering gloves
> Cascading bouquet

Things to Consider: When selecting your bridal gown, keep in mind the time of year and formality of your wedding. It is a good idea to look at bridal magazines to compare the various styles and colors. If you see a gown you like, call boutiques in your area to see if they carry that line. Always try on the gown before ordering it.

When ordering a gown, make sure you order the correct size. If you are between sizes, order the larger one. You can always have your gown tailored down to fit, but it is not always possible to have it enlarged or to lose enough weight to fit into it! Don't forget to ask when your gown will arrive, and be sure to get this in writing. The gown should arrive at least six weeks before the wedding so you can have it tailored and select the appropriate accessories to complement it.

It's a good idea to put on "evening" makeup before going to try on dresses – trying on your wedding gown with a plain face is like trying on an evening dress wearing sneakers!

Beware: Some gown manufacturers suggest ordering a size larger than needed. This requires more alterations which may mean extra charges. It is a good idea to locate a few tailors in your area and ask for alteration pricing in advance. Many boutiques offer tailoring services but you will often find a better price by finding an independent tailor specializing in bridal gown alterations. Also, gowns often fail to arrive on time, creating unnecessary stress for you. Be sure to order your gown with enough time to allow for delivery delays. And be sure to check the reputation of the boutique before buying.

Tips to Save Money: Consider renting a gown or buying one secondhand. Renting a gown usually costs about forty to sixty percent of its retail price. Consider this practical option if you are not planning to preserve the gown. The disadvantage of renting, however, is that your options are more limited. Also, a rented gown usually does not fit as well as a custom tailored gown.

Ask about discontinued styles and gowns. Watch for clearances and sales, or buy your gown "off the rack." Restore or refurbish a family heirloom gown. If you have a friend, sister, or other family member who is planning a wedding, consider purchasing a gown that you could both wear. Change the veil and headpiece to personalize it.

Price Range: $500 - $10,000

ALTERATIONS

Alterations may be necessary in order to make your gown fit perfectly and conform smoothly to your body.

Things to Consider: Alterations usually require several fittings. Allow four to six weeks for alterations to be completed. However, do not alter your gown months before the wedding. Your weight may fluctuate during the final weeks of planning and the gown might not fit properly. Alterations are usually not included in the cost of the gown.

You may also want to consider making some modifications to your gown such as shortening or lengthening the train, customizing the sleeves, beading, and so forth. Ask your bridal boutique what they charge for the modifications you are considering.

Tips to Save Money: Consider hiring an independent tailor. Their fees are usually lower than bridal boutiques.

Price Range: $75 - $500

HEADPIECE/VEIL

The headpiece is the part of the bride's outfit to which the veil is attached.

Options for Headpieces: Banana Clip, Bow, Garden Hat, Headband, Juliet Cap, Mantilla, Pillbox, Pouf, Snood, Tiara.

Options for Veils: Ballet, Bird Cage, Blusher, Cathedral Length, Chapel Length, Fingertip, Flyaway.

ATTIRE

Things to Consider: The headpiece should complement, but not overshadow your gown. In addition to the headpiece, you might want a veil. Veils come in different styles and lengths.

Select a length which complements the length of your train. Consider the total look you're trying to achieve with your gown, headpiece, veil, and hairstyle. If possible, schedule your hair "test appointment" the day you go veil shopping – you'll be able to see how your veil looks on your hairdo!

Tips to Save Money: Some boutiques offer a free headpiece or veil with the purchase of a gown. Make sure you ask for this before purchasing your gown.

Price Range: $60 - $500

GLOVES

Gloves add a nice touch with either short-sleeved, three-quarter length, or sleeveless gowns.

Options: Gloves come in various styles and lengths. Depending on the length of your sleeves, select gloves that reach above your elbow, just below your elbow, halfway between your wrist and elbow, or only to your wrist. Fingerless mitts are another option that you may want to consider.

Things to Consider: You may want to consider fingerless mitts which allow the groom to place the wedding ring on your ring finger without having to remove your glove. You should not wear gloves if your gown has long sleeves, or if you're planning a small, at-home wedding.

Price Range: $15 - $100

JEWELRY

Jewelry can beautifully accent your dress and be the perfect finishing touch.

Options: Select pieces of jewelry that can be classified as "something old, something new, something borrowed, or something blue" (see page 223.)

Things to Consider: Brides look best with just a few pieces of jewelry – perhaps a string of pearls and earrings with a simple bracelet. Purchase complementary jewelry for your bridesmaids, to match the colors of their dresses. This will give your bridal party a coordinated look.

Price Range: $60 - $2,000

GARTER/STOCKINGS

It is customary for the bride to wear a garter just above the knee on her wedding day. After the bouquet tossing ceremony, the groom takes the garter off the bride's leg. All the single men gather on the dance floor. The groom then tosses the garter to them over his back. According to age-old tradition, whoever catches the garter is the next to be married!

Stockings should be selected with care, especially if the groom will be removing a garter from your leg at the reception. Consider having your maid of honor carry an extra pair, just in case you get a run.

Things to Consider: You will need to choose the proper music for this event. A popular and fun song to play during the garter removal ceremony is "The Stripper," by David Rose.

Price Range: $15 - $60

SHOES

Things to Consider: Make sure you select comfortable shoes that complement your gown and don't forget to break them in well before your wedding day. Tight shoes can make you miserable and ruin your otherwise perfect day!

Price Range: $50 -$500

HAIRDRESSER

Many brides prefer to have their hair professionally arranged with their headpiece the day of the wedding rather than trying to do it themselves.

Things to Consider: Consider having your professional hairdresser experiment with your hair and headpiece before your wedding day so there are no surprises. Most hairdressers will include the cost of a sample session in your package. They will try several styles on you and write down the specifics of each one so that things go quickly and smoothly on your wedding day. On the big day, you can go to the salon or have the stylist meet you at your home or dressing site. Consider having him/her arrange your bridal party's hair for a consistent look.

Tips to Save Money: Negotiate having your hair arranged free of charge or at a discount in exchange for bringing your mother, your fiancé's mother, and your bridal party to the salon.

Price Range: $50 - $200 per person

MAKEUP ARTIST

A professional makeup artist will apply makeup that should last throughout the day and will often provide you with samples for touch-ups.

Things to Consider: It's smart to go for a trial run before the day of the wedding so there are no surprises. You can either go to the salon or have the makeup artist meet you at your home or dressing site. Consider having him/her apply makeup for your mother, your fiancé's mother and your bridesmaids for a consistent look.

When selecting a makeup artist, make sure he or she has been trained in makeup for photography. It is very important to wear the proper amount of makeup for photographs.

Consider having your makeup trial right before your hairdresser trial – that way you'll see how your hair looks with your makeup on. It can make a big difference.

Tips to Save Money: Try to negotiate having your makeup applied free of charge or at a discount in exchange for bringing your mother, your fiancé's mother, and your wedding party to the salon.

Price Range: $30 - $150 per person

MANICURE/PEDICURE

As a final touch, it's nice to have a professional manicure and/or pedicure the day of your wedding.

Things to Consider: Don't forget to bring the appropriate color nail polish with you for your appointment. You can either go to the salon or have the manicurist meet you at your home or dressing site. Consider having him/her give your mother, your fiancé's mother, and your bridesmaids a manicure in the same color.

Tips to Save Money: Try to negotiate getting a manicure or pedicure free of charge or at a discount in exchange for bringing your mother, your fiancé's mother, and your wedding party to the salon.

Price Range: $15 - $75 per person

GROOM'S FORMAL WEAR

The groom should select his formal wear based on the formality of the wedding. For a semi-formal or formal wedding, the groom will need a tuxedo. A tuxedo is the formal jacket worn by men on special or formal occasions. The most popular colors are black, white, and gray.

Options: Use the following guidelines to select customary attire for the groom:

Informal wedding:
Business suit
White dress shirt and tie

Semi-formal daytime:
Formal suit
White dress shirt
Cummerbund or vest
Four-in-hand or bow tie

Semi-formal evening:
Formal suit or dinner jacket
Matching trousers
White shirt
Cummerbund or vest
Black bow tie
Cufflinks and studs

Formal daytime:
Cutaway or stroller jacket
Waistcoat
Striped trousers
White wing-collared shirt
Striped tie
Studs and cufflinks

Formal evening:
Black dinner jacket
Matching trousers
Waistcoat
White tuxedo shirt
Bow tie
Cummerbund or vest
Cufflinks

ATTIRE

Very formal daytime: Cutaway coat
Wing-collared shirt
Ascot
Striped trousers
Cufflinks
Gloves

Very formal evening: Black tailcoat
Matching striped trousers
Bow tie
White wing-collared shirt
Waistcoat
Patent leather shoes
Studs and cufflinks
Gloves

Things to Consider: When selecting your formal wear, keep in mind the formality of your wedding, the time of day, and the bride's gown. Consider darker colors for a fall or winter wedding and lighter colors for a spring or summer wedding. When selecting a place to rent your tuxedo, check the reputation of the shop. Make sure they have a wide variety of makes and styles to choose from.

Reserve tuxedos for yourself and your ushers several weeks before the wedding to ensure a wide selection and to allow enough time for alterations. Plan to pick up the tuxedos a few days before the wedding to allow time for last minute alterations in case they don't fit properly. Out-of-town men in your wedding party can be sized at any tuxedo shop. They can send their measurements to you or directly to the shop where you are going to rent your tuxedos.

Ask about the store's return policy and be sure you delegate to the appropriate person (usually your best man) the responsibility of returning all tuxedos within the time allotted. Ushers customarily pay for their own tuxedos.

Tips to Save Money: Try to negotiate getting your tuxedo for free or at a discount in exchange for having your father, your fiancé's father, and ushers rent their tuxedos at that shop.

Price Range: $60 - $200

BRIDAL ATTIRE CHECKLIST

ITEM	Description	Source
Full Slip		
Garter		
Gloves		
Gown		
Handbag		
Jewelry		
Lingerie		
Panty Hose		
Petticoat or Slip		
Shoes		
Something Old		
Something New		
Something Borrowed		
Something Blue		
Stockings		
Veil/Hat		
Other:		
Other:		
Other:		
Other:		
Other:		
Other:		
Other:		

BRIDAL BOUTIQUE COMPARISON CHART

QUESTIONS	POSSIBILITY 1
What is the name of the bridal boutique?	
What is the website and e-mail of the bridal boutique?	
What is the address of the bridal boutique?	
What is the name and phone number of my contact person?	
What are your hours of operation? Are appointments needed?	
What major bridal gown lines do you carry?	
Do you carry outfits for the mother of the bride?	
Do you carry bridesmaids gowns and/or tuxedos?	
Do you carry outfits for the flower girl and ring bearer?	
What is the cost of the desired bridal gown? Do you offer any discounts? Give-aways?	
What is the cost of the desired headpiece?	
Do you offer in-house alterations? If so, what are your fees?	
Do you carry bridal shoes? What is their price range?	
Do you dye shoes to match outfits?	
Do you rent bridal slips? If so, what is the rental fee?	
What is the estimated date of delivery for my gown?	
What is your payment/cancellation policy?	

BRIDAL BOUTIQUE COMPARISON CHART

POSSIBILITY 2	POSSIBILITY 3

BRIDAL ATTIRE

BRIDAL ATTIRE

Bridal Boutique:

Date Ordered:

Salesperson:

Phone Number:

Address:

City: State: Zip Code:

Website:

E-mail:

Description of Dress:

	Manufacturer	Style	Size	Cost	Date Ready/ Ship Date
Wedding Gown					
Headpiece					
Veil/Hat					
Shoes					

GOWN ALTERATIONS

Location:

Cost:

Tailor:

Phone Number:

Address:

City: State: Zip Code:

Website:

E-mail:

	Date	Time
First Alteration		
Second Alteration		
Third Alteration		
Final Alteration		

BRIDESMAIDS' ATTIRE

Bridal Boutique:

Date Ordered:

Salesperson:

Phone Number:

Address:

City: State: Zip Code:

Website:

E-mail:

Description of Dress:

Cost:

Manufacturer:

Date Ready/Ship Date:

BRIDESMAIDS' SIZES

Name	Dress	Head	Weight	Height	Waist	Gloves	Shoes	Hose

GROOM & GROOMSMEN'S ATTIRE

GROOM & GROOMSMEN'S ATTIRE

Store Name:

Date Ordered:

Salesperson:

Phone Number:

Address:

City: State: Zip Code:

Website:

E-mail:

Description of Tuxedo:

Cost:

Manufacturer:

Date Ready:

GROOM & GROOMSMEN'S SIZES

Name	Height	Weight	Waist	Sleeve	Inseam	Jacket	Neck	Shoes

PHOTOGRAPHY

THE PHOTOGRAPHS TAKEN AT YOUR WEDDING ARE THE BEST way to preserve your special day. Chances are you and your fiancé will look at the photos many times during your lifetime. Therefore, hiring a good photographer is one of the most important tasks in planning your wedding.

BRIDE & GROOM'S ALBUM

Options: There are a large variety of wedding albums. They vary in size, color, material, construction, and price. Find one that you like and will feel proud of showing to your friends and family. Some of the most popular manufacturers of wedding albums are Art Leather, Leather Craftsman, and Renaissance.

Make sure you review the differences between these albums before selecting one. You will also need to select the finish process of your photos. Ask your photographer to show you samples of various finishes. Some of the most popular finishes are glossy, luster, semi-matte, pebble finish, spray texture, and oil.

Things to Consider: Make sure you hire a photographer who specializes in weddings. Your photographer should be experienced in wedding procedures and familiar with your ceremony and reception sites. This will allow him/her to anticipate your next move and be in the proper place at the right time to capture all the special moments. Personal rapport is extremely important.

The photographer may be an expert, but if you don't feel comfortable or at ease with him or her, your photography will reflect this. Comfort and compatibility with your photographer can make or break your wedding day and your photographs!

Look at his/her work. See if the photographer captured the excitement and emotion of the bridal couple. Also, remember that the wedding album should unfold like a storybook -- the story of your wedding. Be sure to discuss with your photographer the photos you want so that there is no mis-understanding. A good wedding photographer should have a list of suggested poses to choose from. Use the forms on pages 74-76 to select photos you must have. Give a copy of this form to your photographer.

Look at albums ready to be delivered, or proofs of weddings recently photographed by your photographer. Notice the photographer's preferred style. Some photographers are known for formal poses, while others specialize in more candid, creative shots. Some can do both.

PHOTOGRAPHY

When asked to provide references, many photographers will give you the names of people they know are happy with their work. Some may even give you names from weddings they performed several years ago. This may not indicate the photographer's current ability or reputation. So when asking for references, be sure to ask for recent weddings the photographer has performed. This will give you a good idea of his/her current work. Be sure to ask if the photographer was prompt, cordial, properly dressed, and whether s/he performed his/her duties as expected.

When comparing prices, consider the number, size, and finish of the photographs and the type of album the photographer will use. Ask how many proofs you will get to choose from. The more proofs, the better the selection you will have. Some photographers do not work with proofs. Rather, they simply supply you with a finished album after the wedding. Doing this may reduce the cost of your album but will also reduce your selection of photographs.

Many photographers are switching to digital format cameras. This can be great, because it makes it easy to switch between black and white and color without having to replace rolls of films or use multiple cameras. You may also get a lot more images to choose from, as photographers using a digital camera can shoot far more pictures and take more chances than a photographer shooting with film.

Beware: Make sure the photographer you interview is the one who will actually photograph your wedding. There are many companies with more than one photographer. Often these companies use the work of the best photographer to sell their packages and then send a less experienced photographer to the wedding. Don't get caught in this trap! Be sure you meet with the photographer who will shoot your wedding. That way you can get an idea of his/her style and personality.

Also, some churches do not allow photographs to be shot during the ceremony. Make sure your photographer understands the rules and regulations of your church before planning the ceremony shots.

Tips to Save Money: Consider hiring a professional photographer for the formal shots of your ceremony only. You can then place disposable cameras on each table at the reception and let your guests take candid shots. This will save you a considerable amount of money in photography.

You can also lower the price of your album by paying for the photographs and then putting them into the album yourself. This is a very time-consuming task, so your photographer may reduce the price of his/her package if you opt to do this. To really save money, select a photographer who charges a flat fee to shoot the wedding and allows you to purchase the film.

Compare at least three photographers for quality, value, and price. Photographers who shoot weddings "on the side" are usually less expensive, but the quality of their photographs may not be as good. Select less 8" x 10"s for your album and more 4" x 5"s, and choose a moderately priced album. Ask for specials and package deals.

Price Range: $900 - $9,000

PARENTS' ALBUM

The parents' album is a smaller version of the bride and groom's album. It usually contains about twenty 5" x 7" photographs. Photos should be carefully selected for each individual family. If given as a gift, the album can be personalized with the bride and groom's names and date of their wedding on the front cover.

Tips to Save Money: Try to negotiate at least one free parents' album with the purchase of the bride and groom's album.

Price Range: $100 - $600

EXTRA PRINTS

Extra prints are photographs ordered in addition to the main album or parents' albums. These are usually purchased as gifts for the bridal party, close friends, and family members.

Things to Consider: It is important to discuss the cost of extra prints with your photographer since prices vary considerably. Some photographers offer the main album at great bargains to get the job, but then charge a fortune on extra prints. Think about how many extra prints you would like to order and figure this into your budget before selecting a photographer.

Tips to Save Money: If you can wait, consider not ordering any reprints during the first few years after the wedding. A few years later, contact the photographer and ask if s/he will sell you the negatives. Most photographers will be glad to sell them at a bargain price at a later date. You can then make as many prints as you wish for a fraction of the cost.

Price Range: (5" x 7") = $5 - $20; (8" x 10") = $15 - $30; (11" x 14") = $30 - 100

PROOFS/PREVIEWS

Proofs/previews are the preliminary prints from which the bride and groom select photographs for their album and their parents' albums. They are normally 5" x 5" in size. With the advent of digital technology, many photographers who shoot with digital cameras make your proofs available online. You (and your guests) can browse the available photographs on the Internet and select the ones you'd like to receive prints of. You can often view your photographs within a few days of the wedding!

Things to Consider: When selecting a package, ask how many proofs the photographer will take. The more proofs, the wider the selection you will have to choose from. For a wide selection, the photographer must take at least 2 to 3 times the number of prints that will go into your album. Digital technology makes this much easier.

Ask the photographer how soon after the wedding you will get your proofs. Request this in writing. The proofs should be ready by the time you get back from your honeymoon. Also request to see your proofs before you make the final payment.

Tips to Save Money: Ask your photographer to use your proofs as part of your album package to save developing costs.

Price Range: $100 - $600

NEGATIVES/DIGITAL FILES

Negatives come in different sizes depending on the type of film and equipment used. The most popular film camera for weddings is the medium format camera. When a medium format camera is used, the size of the negatives is 2 1/4" x 2 1/4". When a 35mm camera is used, the negatives are only 1" x 1 1/2". The larger the negative, the higher the quality of the photograph, especially when enlarged. Don't let a photographer convince you that there is no difference in quality between a 35 mm camera and a medium format camera.

The quality of a digital camera's photograph depends on the resolution of the camera. High resolution cameras will produce higher quality images, especially if you need to print large size photographs. Digital cameras do not produce negatives. Images are saved as digital files. These files can be viewed using a computer.

Things to Consider: Many photographers will not sell you the negatives or digital files since they hope to make a profit on selling extra prints after the wedding. Ask the photographers you interview how long they keep the negatives or files and whether they are included in your package. A professional photographer should keep the negatives or files at least five years. Make sure you get this in writing.

Tips to Save Money: If you can wait, consider contacting the photographer a few years later and ask if s/he will sell you the negatives or files at that time. Most photographers will be glad to sell them at a bargain price.

Price Range: $100 - $800

ENGAGEMENT PHOTOGRAPH

The engagement photograph is sent to your local newspapers, along with information announcing your engagement to the public. The bride's parents or her immediate family usually make this announcement.

Things to Consider: You will need to have this photograph taken well in advance of your wedding. Try not to make any drastic changes in appearance (major haircuts) around that time, as you want to look like yourselves!

Tips to Save Money: Look at engagement photographs in your local newspaper. Then have a friend or family member take a photo of you and your fiancé in a pose and with a backdrop similar to the ones you have seen.

Price Range: $75 - $300

FORMAL BRIDAL PORTRAIT

If you intend to announce your marriage in the newspaper the day after your wedding, you will need to have a formal bridal portrait taken several weeks before the wedding. This is a photograph of the bride taken before the wedding in the photographer's studio. This photograph, along with an announcement, must be sent to your local newspapers as soon as possible.

Things to Consider: Some fine bridal salons provide an attractive background where the bride may arrange to have her formal bridal photograph taken after the final fitting of her gown. This will save you the hassle of bringing your gown and headpiece to the photographer's studio and dressing up once again. Consider having your trial makeup and hairstyling appointment the same day that your formal portrait is taken.

Tips to Save Money: If you don't mind announcing your marriage several weeks after the wedding, consider having your formal portrait taken the day of your wedding. This will save you the studio costs, the hassle of getting dressed for the photo, and the photograph will be more natural since the bridal bouquet will be the one you carry down the aisle. Also, brides are always most beautiful on their wedding day!

Price Range: $75 - $300

PHOTOGRAPHERS COMPARISON CHART

QUESTIONS	POSSIBILITY 1
What is the name and phone number of the photographer?	
What is the website and e-mail of the photographer?	
What is the address of the photographer?	
How many years of experience do you have as a photographer?	
What percentage of your business is dedicated to weddings?	
Approximately how many weddings have you photographed?	
Are you the person who will photograph my wedding?	
Will you bring an assistant with you to my wedding?	
How do you typically dress for weddings?	
Do you have a professional studio?	
What type of equipment do you use?	
Do you bring backup equipment with you to weddings?	
Do you visit the ceremony/reception sites prior to the wedding?	
Do you have liability insurance?	
Are you skilled in diffused lighting and soft focus?	
Can you take studio portraits?	
Can you retouch negatives/digital files?	

POSSIBILITY 2	POSSIBILITY 3

PHOTOGRAPHERS COMPARISON CHART

QUESTIONS	POSSIBILITY 1
Can negatives/digital files be purchased?	
If so, what is the cost?	
What is the cost of the package I am interested in?	
What is your payment policy?	
What is your cancellation policy?	
Do you offer a money-back guarantee?	
Do you use proofs?	
How many proofs will I get?	
When will I get my proofs?	
When will I get my album?	
What is the cost of an engagement portrait?	
What is the cost of a formal bridal portrait?	
What is the cost of a parent album?	
What is the cost of a 5"x 7" reprint?	
What is the cost of an 8" x 10" reprint?	
What is the cost of an 11" x 14" reprint?	
What is the cost per additional hour of shooting at the wedding?	

PHOTOGRAPHERS COMPARISON CHART

POSSIBILITY 2	POSSIBILITY 3

PHOTOGRAPHER'S INFORMATION

*Make a copy of this form and give it to your photographer
as a reminder of your various events.*

THE WEDDING OF

Bride's Name: _____   Phone Number: _____

Groom's Name: _____   Phone Number: _____

Wedding Date: _____

PHOTOGRAPHER'S COMPANY

Company Name: _____

Address: _____

City: _____   State: _____   Zip Code: _____

Website: _____

E-mail: _____

Photographer's Name: _____   Phone Number: _____

Assistant's Name: _____   Phone Number: _____

ENGAGEMENT PORTRAIT

Date: _____   Time: _____

Location: _____

Address: _____

City: _____   State: _____   Zip Code: _____

BRIDAL PORTRAIT

Date: _____   Time: _____

Location: _____

Address: _____

City: _____   State: _____   Zip Code: _____

PHOTOGRAPHER'S INFORMATION

*Make a copy of this form and give it to your photographer
as a reminder of your various events.*

OTHER EVENTS

Date: Time:

Location:

Address:

City: State: Zip Code:

CEREMONY

Date:

Arrival Time: Departure Time:

Location:

Address:

City: State: Zip Code:

Ceremony Restrictions/Guidelines:

RECEPTION

Date:

Arrival Time: Departure Time:

Location:

Address:

City: State: Zip Code:

Reception Restrictions/Guidelines:

WEDDING PHOTOGRAPHS

Check-off all photographs you would like taken throughout your wedding day, then make a copy of this form and give it to your photographer.

PRE-CEREMONY PHOTOS

❑ Bride leaving her house

❑ Wedding rings with the invitation

❑ Bride getting dressed for the ceremony

❑ Bride looking at her bridal bouquet

❑ Maid of honor putting garter on bride's leg

❑ Bride by herself

❑ Bride with her mother

❑ Bride with her father

❑ Bride with mother and father

❑ Bride with her entire family and/or any combination thereof

❑ Bride with her maid of honor

❑ Bride with her bridesmaids

❑ Bride with the flower girl and/or ring bearer

❑ Bride's mother putting on her corsage

❑ Groom leaving his house

❑ Groom putting on his boutonniere

❑ Groom with his mother

❑ Groom with his father

❑ Groom with mother and father

❑ Groom with his entire family and/or any combination thereof

❑ Groom with his best man

❑ Groom with his ushers

❑ Groom shaking hands with his best man while looking at his watch

❑ Groom with the bride's father

❑ Bride and her father getting out of the limousine

❑ Special members of the family being seated

❑ Groom waiting for the bride before the processional

❑ Bride and her father just before the processional

WEDDING PHOTOGRAPHS

*Check-off all photographs you would like taken throughout your wedding day,
then make a copy of this form and give it to your photographer.*

OTHER PRE-CEREMONY PHOTOS YOU WOULD LIKE

❑ _____
❑ _____
❑ _____
❑ _____
❑ _____

CEREMONY PHOTOGRAPHS

❑   The processional
❑   Bride and groom saying their vows
❑   Bride and groom exchanging rings
❑   Groom kissing the bride at the altar
❑   The recessional

OTHER CEREMONY PHOTOS YOU WOULD LIKE

❑ _____
❑ _____
❑ _____
❑ _____
❑ _____

POST-CEREMONY PHOTOGRAPHS

❑   Bride and groom
❑   Newlyweds with both of their families
❑   Newlyweds with the entire wedding party
❑   Bride and groom signing the marriage certificate
❑   Flowers and other decorations

OTHER POST-CEREMONY PHOTOS YOU WOULD LIKE

❑ _____
❑ _____
❑ _____
❑ _____
❑ _____

WEDDING PHOTOGRAPHS

Check-off all photographs you would like taken throughout your wedding day,
then make a copy of this form and give it to your photographer.

RECEPTION PHOTOGRAPHS

❏ Entrance of newlyweds and wedding party into the reception site
❏ Receiving line
❏ Guests signing the guest book
❏ Toasts
❏ First dance
❏ Bride and her father dancing
❏ Groom and his mother dancing
❏ Bride dancing with groom's father
❏ Groom dancing with bride's mother
❏ Wedding party and guests dancing
❏ Cake table
❏ Cake-cutting ceremony
❏ Couple feeding each other cake
❏ Buffet table and its decoration
❏ Bouquet-tossing ceremony
❏ Garter-tossing ceremony
❏ Musicians
❏ The wedding party table
❏ The family tables
❏ Candid shots of your guests
❏ Bride and groom saying good-bye to their parents
❏ Bride and groom looking back, waving good-bye in the getaway car

OTHER RECEPTION PHOTOS YOU WOULD LIKE

❏ _____
❏ _____
❏ _____
❏ _____
❏ _____
❏ _____
❏ _____
❏ _____
❏ _____

VIDEOGRAPHY

NEXT TO YOUR PHOTO ALBUM, VIDEOGRAPHY IS THE BEST WAY to preserve your wedding memories. Unlike photographs, videography captures the mood of the wedding day in motion and sound. You have the option of selecting one, two, or three cameras. The more cameras used, the more action captured and the more expensive. An experienced videographer, however, can do a good job with just one camera.

MAIN VIDEO

A good videographer is unobtrusive and knows how to capture all the most important moments of your wedding. Cameras no longer have to be giant, bulky things, as many videographers are switching to digital format. Digital technology also now means that you may receive a DVD instead of a video!

You will need to choose the type of video you want – do you want the footage edited down to a 30 minute film, or do you want an "as it happened" replay? You may wish to have both of these so you can see all the details, but have a shorter version that flows nicely as well. Remember, a short format video requires a lot of time in the editing room and will cost considerably more. Your personal film can take as much as 15-30 hours to put together!

Things to Consider: Be sure to hire a videographer who specializes in weddings and ask to see samples of his or her work. Pay particular attention to details such as special effects, titles, and background music. Find out what's included in the cost of your package so there are no surprises at the end!

Beware: As in photography, there are many companies with more than one videographer. These companies may use the work of their best videographer to sell their packages and then send a less experienced videographer to the wedding. Again, don't get caught in this trap! Be sure to interview the videographer who will shoot your wedding so you can get a good idea of his/her style and personality. Ask to see his/her own work.

Tips to Save Money: Compare videographers' quality, value, and price. There is a wide range and the most expensive may not necessarily be the best. One camera is the most cost effective and may be all you need. Consider hiring a company that offers both videography and photography. You may save overall.

Ask a family member or close friend to videotape your wedding. However, realize that without professional equipment and expertise the final product may not be quite the same.

Price Range: $600 - $4,000

TITLES

Titles and subtitles can be edited into your video before or after the filming. Titles are important since twenty years from now you may not remember the exact time of your wedding or the names of your bridal party members. Some videographers charge more for titling. Make sure you discuss this with your videographer and get in writing exactly what titles will be included.

Options: Titles may include the date, time and location of the wedding, the bride and groom's names, and names of special family members and/or the bridal party. Titles may also include special thanks to those who helped with the wedding. You can then send these people a copy of your video after the wedding, which would be a very appropriate and inexpensive gift!

Tips to Save Money: Consider asking for limited titles, such as only the names of the bride and groom and the date and time of the wedding.

Price Range: $50 - $300

EXTRA HOURS

Find out how much your videographer would charge to stay longer than contracted for in case your reception lasts longer than expected. Don't forget to get this in writing.

Tips to Save Money: Avoid paying extra hours beyond what's included in your selected package. You can do this by calculating the number of hours you think you'll need and negotiating that into your package price. Consider taping the ceremony only.

Price Range: $35 - $150/hour

PHOTO MONTAGE

A photo montage is a series of photographs set to music on video. The number of photographs depends on the length of the songs and the amount of time allotted for each photograph. A typical song usually allows for approximately 30 to 40 photographs. Photo montages are a great way to display and reproduce your photographs. Copies of this video can be made for considerably less than the cost of reproducing photographs.

Options: Photo montages can include photos of you and your fiancé growing up, the rehearsal, the wedding day, the honeymoon, or any combination thereof.

Things to Consider: Send copies of your photo montage video to close friends and family members as a mementos of your wedding.

Tips to Save Money: Consider making a photo montage yourself. This is very easily done with any video camera, a tripod, and a good stereo. The secret is in holding the camera very still and having the proper lighting while videotaping the photographs. Digital technology has made this even easier; with easy-to-use software you can create a beautiful, professional-looking photo montage that can be saved onto a recordable CD and transferred onto video or DVD in a studio. If you own a DVD-recorder, you can make your own copies!

Price Range: $60 - $300

EXTRA COPIES

A professional videographer can reproduce your video much better than you can. Ask your videographer how much s/he charges. You'll certainly want to give your parents a copy!

Tips to Save Money: Borrow a VCR from a friend and make copies yourself. Before considering this, be sure to ask your videographer if that is acceptable – many contracts prohibit this and doing this could be copyright infringement, as with copying any tape.

Price Range: $15 - $50

VIDEOGRAPHY COMPARISON CHART

QUESTIONS	POSSIBILITY 1
What is the name and phone number of the videographer?	
What is the website and e-mail address of the videographer?	
What is the address of the videographer?	
How many years of experience do you have as a videographer?	
Approximately how many weddings have you videotaped?	
Are you the person who will videotape my wedding?	
Will you bring an assistant with you to my wedding?	
What type of equipment do you use? Do you have a wireless microphone?	
What format do you use (VHS, digital)? Do you bring backup equipment with you?	
Do you visit the ceremony and reception sites before the wedding?	
Do you edit the tape after the event? Who keeps the raw footage?	
When will I receive the final product?	
Cost of the desired package? What does it include?	
Can you make a photo montage? If so, what is your price?	
What is your payment policy?	
What is your cancellation policy?	
Do you offer a money-back guarantee?	

VIDEOGRAPHY COMPARISON CHART

POSSIBILITY 2	POSSIBILITY 3

NOTES

_____

_____

_____

_____

_____

_____

_____

_____

_____

_____

_____

_____

_____

_____

_____

_____

_____

_____

_____

_____

_____

_____

_____

_____

_____

_____

_____

_____

_____

STATIONERY

BEGIN CREATING YOUR GUEST LIST AS SOON AS POSSIBLE. Ask your parents and the groom's parents for a list of people they would like to invite. You and your fiancé should make your own lists. Make certain that all names are spelled correctly and that all addresses are current. Determine if you wish to include children; if so, add their names to your list. All children over the age of 16 should receive their own invitation.

INVITATIONS

Order your invitations at least four months before the wedding. Allow an additional month for engraved invitations. Invitations are traditionally issued by the bride's parents; if the groom's parents are assuming some of the wedding expenses, the invitations should be in their names also. Mail all invitations at the same time, six to eight weeks before the wedding.

Options: There are three types of invitations: traditional/formal, contemporary, and informal. The traditional/formal wedding invitation is white, soft cream, or ivory with raised black lettering. The printing is done on the top page of a double sheet of thick quality paper; the inside is left blank. The contemporary invitation is typically an individualized presentation that makes a statement about the bride and groom.

Informal invitations are often printed on the front of a single, heavyweight card and may be handwritten or preprinted.

There are three types of printing: engraved, thermography, and offset printing. Engraving is the most expensive, traditional, and formal type of printing. It also takes the longest to complete. In engraved printing, stationery is pressed onto a copper plate, which makes the letters rise slightly from the page. Thermography is a process that fuses powder and ink to create a raised letter. This takes less time than engraving and is less expensive because copper plates do not have to be engraved. Offset printing, the least expensive, is the quickest to produce and offers a variety of styles and colors. It is also the least formal.

Things to Consider: If all your guests are to be invited to both the ceremony and the reception, a combined invitation may be sent without separate enclosure cards. Order one invitation for each married or co-habiting couple that you plan to invite. The officiant and his/her spouse as well as your attendants should receive an invitation.

STATIONERY

Order approximately 20% more stationery than your actual count. Allow a minimum of two weeks to address and mail the invitations, longer if using a calligrapher or if your guest list is very large. You may also want to consider ordering invitations to the rehearsal dinner, as these should be in the same style as the wedding invitation.

SAMPLES OF TRADITIONAL/FORMAL INVITATIONS

1) When the bride's parents sponsor the wedding:

Mr. and Mrs. Alexander Waterman Smith
request the honor of your presence
at the marriage of their daughter
Carol Ann
to
Mr. William James Clark
on Saturday, the fifth of August
two thousand six
at two o'clock in the afternoon
Saint James by-the-Sea
La Jolla, California

2) When the groom's parents sponsor the wedding:

Mr. and Mrs. Michael Burdell Clark
request the honor of your presence
at the marriage of
Miss Carol Ann Smith
to their son
Mr. William James Clark

3) When both the bride and groom's parents sponsor the wedding:

Mr. and Mrs. Alexander Waterman Smith
and
Mr. and Mrs. Michael Burdell Clark
request the honor of your presence
at the marriage of their children
Miss Carol Ann Smith
to
Mr. William James Clark

OR

Mr. and Mrs. Alexander Waterman Smith
request the honor of your presence
at the marriage of their daughter
Carol Ann Smith
to
William James Clark
son of Mr. and Mrs. Michael Burdell Clark

4) When the bride and groom sponsor their own wedding:

The honor of your presence is requested
at the marriage of
Miss Carol Ann Smith
and
Mr. William James Clark

OR

Miss Carol Ann Smith
and
Mr. William James Clark
request the honor of your presence
at their marriage

5) With divorced or deceased parents:

a) When the bride's mother is sponsoring the wedding and is not remarried:

Mrs. Julie Hurden Smith
requests the honor of your presence
at the marriage of her daughter
Carol Ann

b) When the bride's mother is sponsoring the wedding and has remarried:

Mrs. Julie Hurden Booker
requests the honor of your presence
at the marriage of her daughter
Carol Ann Smith

OR

Mr. and Mrs. John Thomas Booker
request the honor of your presence
at the marriage of Mrs. Booker's daughter
Carol Ann Smith

c) When the bride's father is sponsoring the wedding and has not remarried:

Mr. Alexander Waterman Smith
requests the honor of your presence
at the marriage of his daughter
Carol Ann

d) When the bride's father is sponsoring the wedding and has remarried:

Mr. and Mrs. Alexander Waterman Smith
request the honor of your presence
at the marriage of Mr. Smith's daughter
Carol Ann

6) With deceased parents:

a) When a close friend or relative sponsors the wedding:

Mr. and Mrs. Brandt Elliott Lawson
request the honor of your presence
at the marriage of their granddaughter
Carol Ann Smith

7) In military ceremonies, the rank determines the placement of names:

a) Any title lower than sergeant should be omitted. Only the branch of
service should be included under that person's name:

Mr. and Mrs. Alexander Waterman Smith
request the honor of your presence
at the marriage of their daughter
Carol Ann
to
William James Clark
United States Army

b) Junior officers' titles are placed below their names and are followed by their branch of service:

Mr. and Mrs. Alexander Waterman Smith
request the honor of your presence
at the marriage of their daughter
Carol Ann
to
William James Clark
First Lieutenant, United States Army

c) If the rank is higher than lieutenant, titles are placed before names, and the branch of service is placed on the following line:

Mr. and Mrs. Alexander Waterman Smith
request the honor of your presence
at the marriage of their daughter
Carol Ann
to
Captain William James Clark
United States Navy

SAMPLE OF A LESS FORMAL/MORE CONTEMPORARY INVITATION

Mr. and Mrs. Alexander Waterman Smith
would like you to
join with their daughter
Carol Ann
and
William James Clark
in the celebration of their marriage

Tips to Save Money: Thermography looks like engraving and is one-third the cost. Choose paper stock that is reasonable and yet achieves your overall look. Select invitations that can be mailed using just one stamp. Order at least 25 extra invitations in case you soil some or add people to your list. To reorder this small number of invitations later would cost nearly three times the amount you'll spend up front.

Price Range: $0.75 - $6.00 per invitation

STATIONERY

RESPONSE CARDS

Response cards are enclosed with the invitation to determine the number of people who will be attending your wedding. They are the smallest card size accepted by the postal service and should be printed in the same style as the invitation. An invitation to only the wedding ceremony does not usually include a request for a reply. However, response cards should be used when it is necessary to have an exact head-count for special seating arrangements. Response cards are widely accepted today. If included, these cards should be easy for your guests to understand and use. Include a self-addressed and stamped return envelope to make it easy for your guests to return the response cards.

Things to Consider: You should not include a line that reads "number of persons" on your response cards because only those whose names appear on the inner and outer envelopes are invited. Each couple, each single person, and all children over the age of 16 should receive their own invitation. Indicate on the inner envelope if they may bring an escort or guest. The omitting of children's names from the inner envelope infers that the children are not invited.

Samples of wording for response cards:

M_____

(The M may be eliminated from the line, especially if many Drs. are invited)

____ accepts

____ regrets

Saturday the fifth of July

Oceanside Country Club

OR

The favor of your reply is requested

by the twenty-second of May

M_____

will _____ attend

Price Range: $0.40 - $1.00 each

RECEPTION CARDS

If the guest list for the ceremony is larger than that for the reception, a separate card with the date, time, and location for the reception should be enclosed with the ceremony invitation for those guests also invited to the reception. Reception cards should be placed in front of the invitation, facing the back flap and the person inserting them. They should be printed on the same quality paper and in the same style as the invitation itself.

Sample of a formally-worded reception card:

> Mr. and Mrs. Alexander Waterman Smith
> request the pleasure of your company
> Saturday, the third of July
> at three o'clock
> Oceanside Country Club
> 2020 Waterview Lane
> Oceanside, California

Sample of a less formal reception card:

> Reception immediately following the ceremony
> Oceanside Country Club
> 2020 Waterview Lane
> Oceanside, California

Things to Consider: You may also include a reception card in all your invitations if the reception is to be held at a different site than the ceremony.

Tips to Save Money: If all people invited to the ceremony are also invited to the reception, include the reception information on the invitation and eliminate the reception card. This will save printing and postage costs.

Price Range: $0.40 - $1.00 each

CEREMONY CARDS

If the guest list for the reception is larger than the guest list for the ceremony, a special insertion card with the date, time, and location for the ceremony should be enclosed with the reception invitation for those guests also invited to the ceremony.

Ceremony cards should be placed in front of the invitation, facing the back flap and the person inserting them. They should be printed on the same quality paper and in the same style as the invitation itself.

Price Range: $0.40 - $1.00 each

STATIONERY

PEW CARDS

Pew cards may be used to let special guests and family members know they are to be seated in the reserved section on either the bride's side or the groom's side. These are most typically seen in large, formal ceremonies. Guests should take this card to the ceremony and show it to the ushers, who should then escort them to their seats.

Options: Pew cards may indicate a specific pew number if specific seats are assigned, or may read "Within the Ribbon" if certain pews are reserved but no specific seat is assigned.

Things to Consider: Pew cards may be inserted along with the invitation, or may be sent separately after the RSVPs have been returned. It is often easier to send them after you have received all RSVPs so you know how many reserved pews will be needed.

Tips to Save Money: Include the pew card with the invitation to special guests and just say "Within the Ribbon." After you have received all your RSVPs, you will know how many pews need to be reserved. This will save you the cost of mailing the pew cards separately.

Price Range: $0.25 - $1.00 each

SEATING/PLACE CARDS

Seating/place cards are used to let guests know where they should be seated at the reception and are a good way of putting people together so they feel most comfortable. Place cards should be laid out alphabetically on a table at the entrance to the reception. Each card should correspond to a table – either by number, color, or other identifying factor. Each table should be marked accordingly.

Options: Select a traditional or contemporary design for your place cards, depending on the style of your wedding. Regardless of the design, place cards must contain the same information: the bride and groom's names on the first line; the date on the second line; the third line is left blank for you to write in the guest's name; and the fourth line is for the table number, color, or other identifying factor.

Price Range: $0.25 - $1.00 each

RAIN CARDS

These cards are enclosed when guests are invited to an outdoor ceremony and/or reception, informing them of an alternate location in case of bad weather. As with other enclosures, rain cards should be placed in front of the invitation, facing the back flap and the person inserting them. They should be printed on the same quality paper and in the same style as the invitation itself.

Price Range: $0.25 - $1.00 each

MAPS

Maps to the ceremony and/or reception are becoming frequent inserts in wedding invitations. They need to be drawn and printed in the same style as the invitation and are usually on a small, heavier card. If they are not printed in the same style or on the same type of paper as the invitation, they should be mailed separately.

Options: Maps should include both written and visual instructions, keeping in mind the fact that guests may be coming from different locations.

Things to Consider: Order extra maps to hand out at the ceremony if the reception is at a different location.

Tips to Save Money: If you are comfortable with computers, you can purchase software that allows you to draw your own maps. Print a map to both the ceremony and reception on the same sheet of paper, perhaps one on each side. This will save you the cost of mailing two maps. Or have your ushers hand out maps to the reception after the ceremony.

Price Range: $0.50 - $1.00 each

CEREMONY PROGRAMS

Ceremony programs are printed documents showing the sequence of events during the ceremony. These programs add a personal touch to your wedding and are a convenient way of letting guests know who your attendants, officiant, and ceremony musicians are.

Options: Ceremony programs can be handed out by the ushers, or they can be placed at the back of the church for guests to take as they enter.

Price Range: $0.75 - $3.00 each

STATIONERY

ANNOUNCEMENTS

Announcements are not obligatory but serve a useful purpose. They may be sent to friends who are not invited to the wedding because the number of guests must be limited, or because they live too far away. They may also be sent to acquaintances who, while not particularly close to the family, might still wish to know about the marriage.

Announcements are also appropriate for friends and acquaintances who are not expected to attend and for whom you do not want to give an obligation of sending a gift. They should include the day, month, year, city, and state where the ceremony took place.

Things to Consider: Announcements should never be sent to anyone who has received an invitation to the ceremony or the reception. They are printed on the same paper and in the same style as the invitation. They should be addressed before the wedding and mailed the day of or the day after the ceremony.

Price Range: $0.75 - $2.00 each

THANK-YOU NOTES

Regardless of whether the bride has thanked the donor in person or not, she must write a thank-you note for every gift received.

Things to Consider: Order thank-you notes along with your other stationery at least four months before your wedding. You should order some with your maiden initials for thank-you notes sent before the ceremony, and the rest with your married initials for notes sent after the wedding and for future use. Send thank-you notes within two weeks of receiving a gift that arrives before the wedding, and within two months after the honeymoon for gifts received on or after your wedding day. Be sure to mention the gift you received in the body of the note and let the person know how much you like it and what you plan to do with it.

Price Range: $0.40 - $0.75 each

STAMPS

Don't forget to budget stamps for response cards as well as for invitations!

Things to Consider: Don't order stamps until you have had the post office weigh your completed invitation. It may exceed the size and weight for one stamp. Order commemorative stamps that fit the occasion.

Price Range: $0.39 - $1.00 per invitation

CALLIGRAPHY

Calligraphy is a form of elegant handwriting often used to address invitations for formal occasions. Traditional wedding invitations should be addressed in black or blue fountain pen.

Options: You may address the invitations yourself, hire a professional calligrapher, or have your invitations addressed using calligraphy by computer. Make sure you use the same method or person to address both the inner and outer envelopes.

Tips to Save Money: You may want to consider taking a short course to learn the art of calligraphy so that you can address your own invitations. If you have a computer with a laser printer, you can address the invitations yourself using one of many beautiful calligraphy fonts.

Price Range: $0.50 - $3.00 each

NAPKINS/MATCHBOOKS

Napkins and matchbooks may also be ordered from your stationer. These are placed around the reception room as decorative items and mementos of the event.

Things to Consider: Napkins and matchbooks can be printed in your wedding colors, or simply white with gold or silver lettering. Include both of your names and the wedding date. You may consider including a phrase or thought, or a small graphic design above your names.

Price Range: $0.50 - $1.50 each

NOTES

STATIONERY ITEM	Quantity	Cost
❑ Invitations		
❑ Envelopes		
❑ Response Cards/Envelopes		
❑ Reception Cards		
❑ Ceremony Cards		
❑ Pew Cards		
❑ Seating/Place Cards		
❑ Rain Cards		
❑ Maps		
❑ Ceremony Programs		
❑ Announcements		
❑ Thank-You Notes		
❑ Stamps		
❑ Napkins/Matchbooks		
❑ Other		
❑ Other		
❑ Other		
❑ Other		

The Marriage of
Carol Ann Smith and William James Clark
the eleventh of March, 2008
San Diego, California

OUR CEREMONY

Prelude:
All I Ask of You, by Andrew Lloyd Webber

Processional:
Canon in D Major, by Pachelbel

Rite of Marriage

Welcome guests

Statement of intentions

Marriage vows

Exchange of rings

Blessing of bride and groom

Pronouncement of marriage

Presentation of the bride and groom

Recessional:
Trumpet Voluntary, by Jeromiah Clarke

OUR WEDDING PARTY

Maid of Honor:
Susan Smith, Sister of Bride

Best Man:
Brandt Clark, Brother of Groom

Bridesmaids:
Janet Anderson, Friend of Bride
Lisa Bennett, Friend of Bride

Ushers:
Mark Gleason, Friend of Groom
Tommy Olson, Friend of Groom

Officiant:
Father Henry Thomas

OUR RECEPTION

Please join us after the ceremony
in the celebration of our marriage at:
La Valencia Hotel
1132 Prospect Street
La Jolla, California

STATIONERY COMPARISON CHART

QUESTIONS	POSSIBILITY 1
What is the name and phone number of the stationery provider?	
What is the website and e-mail of the stationery provider?	
What is the address of the stationery provider?	
How many years of experience do you have?	
What lines of stationery do you carry?	
What types of printing process do you offer?	
How soon in advance does the order have to be placed?	
What is the turn around time?	
What is the cost of the desired announcement?	
What is the cost of the desired invitation?	
What is the cost of the desired response card? Reception card?	
What is the cost of the desired thank-you note?	
What is the cost of the desired personalized party favors, i.e. matchbooks, napkins, etc.?	
What is the cost of the desired wedding program?	
What is the cost of addressing the envelopes in calligraphy?	
What is your payment policy?	
What is your cancellation policy?	

STATIONERY COMPARISON CHART

POSSIBILITY 2	POSSIBILITY 3

STATIONERY DESCRIPTION

STATIONER:

Date Ordered:

Sales Person: Phone Number:

Address:

City: State: Zip Code:

Website:

E-mail:

Invitations (Paper, Style, Color, Font, Printing):

Reception Cards (Paper, Style, Color, Font, Printing):

Response Cards (Paper, Style, Color, Font, Printing):

Announcements (Paper, Style, Color, Font, Printing):

Seating/Pew Cards (Paper, Style, Color, Font, Printing):

Napkins/Matchbooks (Paper, Style, Color, Font, Printing):

Invitations:

Announcements:

Reception Cards:

Response Cards:

Seating/Pew Cards:

Napkins/Matchbooks:

GUEST AND GIFT LIST

Make as many copies of this form as needed.

Name:

Address:

City:

State: Zip Code:

Phone Number:

E-mail:

Table#   Pew#

Shower Gift:

❏ Thank You Note Sent

Wedding Gift:

❏ Thank You Note Sent

Name:

Address:

City:

State: Zip Code:

Phone Number:

E-mail:

Table#   Pew#

Shower Gift:

❏ Thank You Note Sent

Wedding Gift:

❏ Thank You Note Sent

Name:

Address:

City:

State: Zip Code:

Phone Number:

E-mail:

Table#   Pew#

Shower Gift:

❏ Thank You Note Sent

Wedding Gift:

❏ Thank You Note Sent

Name:

Address:

City:

State: Zip Code:

Phone Number:

E-mail:

Table#   Pew#

Shower Gift:

❏ Thank You Note Sent

Wedding Gift:

❏ Thank You Note Sent

Name:

Address:

City:

State: Zip Code:

Phone Number:

E-mail:

Table#   Pew#

Shower Gift:

❏ Thank You Note Sent

Wedding Gift:

❏ Thank You Note Sent

Name:

Address:

City:

State: Zip Code:

Phone Number:

E-mail:

Table#   Pew#

Shower Gift:

❏ Thank You Note Sent

Wedding Gift:

❏ Thank You Note Sent

Make as many copies of this form as needed.

Name:

Address:

City:

State: Zip Code:

Phone Number:

E-mail:

Table#   Pew#

Shower Gift:

❑ Thank You Note Sent

Wedding Gift:

❑ Thank You Note Sent

Name:

Address:

City:

State: Zip Code:

Phone Number:

E-mail:

Table#   Pew#

Shower Gift:

❑ Thank You Note Sent

Wedding Gift:

❑ Thank You Note Sent

Name:

Address:

City:

State: Zip Code:

Phone Number:

E-mail:

Table#   Pew#

Shower Gift:

❑ Thank You Note Sent

Wedding Gift:

❑ Thank You Note Sent

Name:

Address:

City:

State: Zip Code:

Phone Number:

E-mail:

Table#   Pew#

Shower Gift:

❑ Thank You Note Sent

Wedding Gift:

❑ Thank You Note Sent

Name:

Address:

City:

State: Zip Code:

Phone Number:

E-mail:

Table#   Pew#

Shower Gift:

❑ Thank You Note Sent

Wedding Gift:

❑ Thank You Note Sent

Name:

Address:

City:

State: Zip Code:

Phone Number:

E-mail:

Table#   Pew#

Shower Gift:

❑ Thank You Note Sent

Wedding Gift:

❑ Thank You Note Sent

GUEST AND GIFT LIST

Make as many copies of this form as needed.

Name:

Address:

City:

State: Zip Code:

Phone Number:

E-mail:

Table#   Pew#

Shower Gift:

❑ Thank You Note Sent

Wedding Gift:

❑ Thank You Note Sent

Name:

Address:

City:

State: Zip Code:

Phone Number:

E-mail:

Table#   Pew#

Shower Gift:

❑ Thank You Note Sent

Wedding Gift:

❑ Thank You Note Sent

Name:

Address:

City:

State: Zip Code:

Phone Number:

E-mail:

Table#   Pew#

Shower Gift:

❑ Thank You Note Sent

Wedding Gift:

❑ Thank You Note Sent

Name:

Address:

City:

State: Zip Code:

Phone Number:

E-mail:

Table#   Pew#

Shower Gift:

❑ Thank You Note Sent

Wedding Gift:

❑ Thank You Note Sent

Name:

Address:

City:

State: Zip Code:

Phone Number:

E-mail:

Table#   Pew#

Shower Gift:

❑ Thank You Note Sent

Wedding Gift:

❑ Thank You Note Sent

Name:

Address:

City:

State: Zip Code:

Phone Number:

E-mail:

Table#   Pew#

Shower Gift:

❑ Thank You Note Sent

Wedding Gift:

❑ Thank You Note Sent

Make as many copies of this form as needed.

Name:

Address:

City:

State: Zip Code:

Phone Number:

E-mail:

Table#   Pew#

Shower Gift:

❑ Thank You Note Sent

Wedding Gift:

❑ Thank You Note Sent

Name:

Address:

City:

State: Zip Code:

Phone Number:

E-mail:

Table#   Pew#

Shower Gift:

❑ Thank You Note Sent

Wedding Gift:

❑ Thank You Note Sent

Name:

Address:

City:

State: Zip Code:

Phone Number:

E-mail:

Table#   Pew#

Shower Gift:

❑ Thank You Note Sent

Wedding Gift:

❑ Thank You Note Sent

Name:

Address:

City:

State: Zip Code:

Phone Number:

E-mail:

Table#   Pew#

Shower Gift:

❑ Thank You Note Sent

Wedding Gift:

❑ Thank You Note Sent

Name:

Address:

City:

State: Zip Code:

Phone Number:

E-mail:

Table#   Pew#

Shower Gift:

❑ Thank You Note Sent

Wedding Gift:

❑ Thank You Note Sent

Name:

Address:

City:

State: Zip Code:

Phone Number:

E-mail:

Table#   Pew#

Shower Gift:

❑ Thank You Note Sent

Wedding Gift:

❑ Thank You Note Sent

GUEST AND GIFT LIST

Make as many copies of this form as needed.

Name:

Address:

City:

State: Zip Code:

Phone Number:

E-mail:

Table#   Pew#

Shower Gift:

❑ Thank You Note Sent

Wedding Gift:

❑ Thank You Note Sent

Name:

Address:

City:

State: Zip Code:

Phone Number:

E-mail:

Table#   Pew#

Shower Gift:

❑ Thank You Note Sent

Wedding Gift:

❑ Thank You Note Sent

Name:

Address:

City:

State: Zip Code:

Phone Number:

E-mail:

Table#   Pew#

Shower Gift:

❑ Thank You Note Sent

Wedding Gift:

❑ Thank You Note Sent

Name:

Address:

City:

State: Zip Code:

Phone Number:

E-mail:

Table#   Pew#

Shower Gift:

❑ Thank You Note Sent

Wedding Gift:

❑ Thank You Note Sent

Name:

Address:

City:

State: Zip Code:

Phone Number:

E-mail:

Table#   Pew#

Shower Gift:

❑ Thank You Note Sent

Wedding Gift:

❑ Thank You Note Sent

Name:

Address:

City:

State: Zip Code:

Phone Number:

E-mail:

Table#   Pew#

Shower Gift:

❑ Thank You Note Sent

Wedding Gift:

❑ Thank You Note Sent

GUEST AND GIFT LIST

Make as many copies of this form as needed.

Name:

Address:

City:

State: Zip Code:

Phone Number:

E-mail:

Table#   Pew#

Shower Gift:

❑ Thank You Note Sent

Wedding Gift:

❑ Thank You Note Sent

Name:

Address:

City:

State: Zip Code:

Phone Number:

E-mail:

Table#   Pew#

Shower Gift:

❑ Thank You Note Sent

Wedding Gift:

❑ Thank You Note Sent

Name:

Address:

City:

State: Zip Code:

Phone Number:

E-mail:

Table#   Pew#

Shower Gift:

❑ Thank You Note Sent

Wedding Gift:

❑ Thank You Note Sent

Name:

Address:

City:

State: Zip Code:

Phone Number:

E-mail:

Table#   Pew#

Shower Gift:

❑ Thank You Note Sent

Wedding Gift:

❑ Thank You Note Sent

Name:

Address:

City:

State: Zip Code:

Phone Number:

E-mail:

Table#   Pew#

Shower Gift:

❑ Thank You Note Sent

Wedding Gift:

❑ Thank You Note Sent

Name:

Address:

City:

State: Zip Code:

Phone Number:

E-mail:

Table#   Pew#

Shower Gift:

❑ Thank You Note Sent

Wedding Gift:

❑ Thank You Note Sent

GUEST AND GIFT LIST

Make as many copies of this form as needed.

Name:

Address:

City:

State: Zip Code:

Phone Number:

E-mail:

Table#   Pew#

Shower Gift:

❏ Thank You Note Sent

Wedding Gift:

❏ Thank You Note Sent

Name:

Address:

City:

State: Zip Code:

Phone Number:

E-mail:

Table#   Pew#

Shower Gift:

❏ Thank You Note Sent

Wedding Gift:

❏ Thank You Note Sent

Name:

Address:

City:

State: Zip Code:

Phone Number:

E-mail:

Table#   Pew#

Shower Gift:

❏ Thank You Note Sent

Wedding Gift:

❏ Thank You Note Sent

Name:

Address:

City:

State: Zip Code:

Phone Number:

E-mail:

Table#   Pew#

Shower Gift:

❏ Thank You Note Sent

Wedding Gift:

❏ Thank You Note Sent

Name:

Address:

City:

State: Zip Code:

Phone Number:

E-mail:

Table#   Pew#

Shower Gift:

❏ Thank You Note Sent

Wedding Gift:

❏ Thank You Note Sent

Name:

Address:

City:

State: Zip Code:

Phone Number:

E-mail:

Table#   Pew#

Shower Gift:

❏ Thank You Note Sent

Wedding Gift:

❏ Thank You Note Sent

Make as many copies of this form as needed.

Name:

Address:

City:

State: Zip Code:

Phone Number:

E-mail:

Table#   Pew#

Shower Gift:

❑ Thank You Note Sent

Wedding Gift:

❑ Thank You Note Sent

Name:

Address:

City:

State: Zip Code:

Phone Number:

E-mail:

Table#   Pew#

Shower Gift:

❑ Thank You Note Sent

Wedding Gift:

❑ Thank You Note Sent

Name:

Address:

City:

State: Zip Code:

Phone Number:

E-mail:

Table#   Pew#

Shower Gift:

❑ Thank You Note Sent

Wedding Gift:

❑ Thank You Note Sent

Name:

Address:

City:

State: Zip Code:

Phone Number:

E-mail:

Table#   Pew#

Shower Gift:

❑ Thank You Note Sent

Wedding Gift:

❑ Thank You Note Sent

Name:

Address:

City:

State: Zip Code:

Phone Number:

E-mail:

Table#   Pew#

Shower Gift:

❑ Thank You Note Sent

Wedding Gift:

❑ Thank You Note Sent

Name:

Address:

City:

State: Zip Code:

Phone Number:

E-mail:

Table#   Pew#

Shower Gift:

❑ Thank You Note Sent

Wedding Gift:

❑ Thank You Note Sent

GUEST AND GIFT LIST

Make as many copies of this form as needed.

Name:

Address:

City:

State: Zip Code:

Phone Number:

E-mail:

Table#   Pew#

Shower Gift:

❑ Thank You Note Sent

Wedding Gift:

❑ Thank You Note Sent

Name:

Address:

City:

State: Zip Code:

Phone Number:

E-mail:

Table#   Pew#

Shower Gift:

❑ Thank You Note Sent

Wedding Gift:

❑ Thank You Note Sent

Name:

Address:

City:

State: Zip Code:

Phone Number:

E-mail:

Table#   Pew#

Shower Gift:

❑ Thank You Note Sent

Wedding Gift:

❑ Thank You Note Sent

Name:

Address:

City:

State: Zip Code:

Phone Number:

E-mail:

Table#   Pew#

Shower Gift:

❑ Thank You Note Sent

Wedding Gift:

❑ Thank You Note Sent

Name:

Address:

City:

State: Zip Code:

Phone Number:

E-mail:

Table#   Pew#

Shower Gift:

❑ Thank You Note Sent

Wedding Gift:

❑ Thank You Note Sent

Name:

Address:

City:

State: Zip Code:

Phone Number:

E-mail:

Table#   Pew#

Shower Gift:

❑ Thank You Note Sent

Wedding Gift:

❑ Thank You Note Sent

Make as many copies of this form as needed.

Name:

Address:

City:

State: Zip Code:

Phone Number:

E-mail:

Table#   Pew#

Shower Gift:

❏ Thank You Note Sent

Wedding Gift:

❏ Thank You Note Sent

Name:

Address:

City:

State: Zip Code:

Phone Number:

E-mail:

Table#   Pew#

Shower Gift:

❏ Thank You Note Sent

Wedding Gift:

❏ Thank You Note Sent

Name:

Address:

City:

State: Zip Code:

Phone Number:

E-mail:

Table#   Pew#

Shower Gift:

❏ Thank You Note Sent

Wedding Gift:

❏ Thank You Note Sent

Name:

Address:

City:

State: Zip Code:

Phone Number:

E-mail:

Table#   Pew#

Shower Gift:

❏ Thank You Note Sent

Wedding Gift:

❏ Thank You Note Sent

Name:

Address:

City:

State: Zip Code:

Phone Number:

E-mail:

Table#   Pew#

Shower Gift:

❏ Thank You Note Sent

Wedding Gift:

❏ Thank You Note Sent

Name:

Address:

City:

State: Zip Code:

Phone Number:

E-mail:

Table#   Pew#

Shower Gift:

❏ Thank You Note Sent

Wedding Gift:

❏ Thank You Note Sent

GUEST AND GIFT LIST

Make as many copies of this form as needed.

Name:

Address:

City:

State: Zip Code:

Phone Number:

E-mail:

Table#   Pew#

Shower Gift:

❑ Thank You Note Sent

Wedding Gift:

❑ Thank You Note Sent

Name:

Address:

City:

State: Zip Code:

Phone Number:

E-mail:

Table#   Pew#

Shower Gift:

❑ Thank You Note Sent

Wedding Gift:

❑ Thank You Note Sent

Name:

Address:

City:

State: Zip Code:

Phone Number:

E-mail:

Table#   Pew#

Shower Gift:

❑ Thank You Note Sent

Wedding Gift:

❑ Thank You Note Sent

Name:

Address:

City:

State: Zip Code:

Phone Number:

E-mail:

Table#   Pew#

Shower Gift:

❑ Thank You Note Sent

Wedding Gift:

❑ Thank You Note Sent

Name:

Address:

City:

State: Zip Code:

Phone Number:

E-mail:

Table#   Pew#

Shower Gift:

❑ Thank You Note Sent

Wedding Gift:

❑ Thank You Note Sent

Name:

Address:

City:

State: Zip Code:

Phone Number:

E-mail:

Table#   Pew#

Shower Gift:

❑ Thank You Note Sent

Wedding Gift:

❑ Thank You Note Sent

Make as many copies of this form as needed.

Name:

Address:

City:

State: Zip Code:

Phone Number:

E-mail:

Table#   Pew#

Shower Gift:

❏ Thank You Note Sent

Wedding Gift:

❏ Thank You Note Sent

Name:

Address:

City:

State: Zip Code:

Phone Number:

E-mail:

Table#   Pew#

Shower Gift:

❏ Thank You Note Sent

Wedding Gift:

❏ Thank You Note Sent

Name:

Address:

City:

State: Zip Code:

Phone Number:

E-mail:

Table#   Pew#

Shower Gift:

❏ Thank You Note Sent

Wedding Gift:

❏ Thank You Note Sent

Name:

Address:

City:

State: Zip Code:

Phone Number:

E-mail:

Table#   Pew#

Shower Gift:

❏ Thank You Note Sent

Wedding Gift:

❏ Thank You Note Sent

Name:

Address:

City:

State: Zip Code:

Phone Number:

E-mail:

Table#   Pew#

Shower Gift:

❏ Thank You Note Sent

Wedding Gift:

❏ Thank You Note Sent

Name:

Address:

City:

State: Zip Code:

Phone Number:

E-mail:

Table#   Pew#

Shower Gift:

❏ Thank You Note Sent

Wedding Gift:

❏ Thank You Note Sent

ANNOUNCEMENT LIST

Make as many copies of this form as needed.

Name:

Address:

City:

State: Zip Code:

Phone Number:

E-mail:

Name:

Address:

City:

State: Zip Code:

Phone Number:

E-mail:

Name:

Address:

City:

State: Zip Code:

Phone Number:

E-mail:

Name:

Address:

City:

State: Zip Code:

Phone Number:

E-mail:

Name:

Address:

City:

State: Zip Code:

Phone Number:

E-mail:

Name:

Address:

City:

State: Zip Code:

Phone Number:

E-mail:

Name:

Address:

City:

State: Zip Code:

Phone Number:

E-mail:

Name:

Address:

City:

State: Zip Code:

Phone Number:

E-mail:

Name:

Address:

City:

State: Zip Code:

Phone Number:

E-mail:

Name:

Address:

City:

State: Zip Code:

Phone Number:

E-mail:

Name:

Address:

City:

State: Zip Code:

Phone Number:

E-mail:

Name:

Address:

City:

State: Zip Code:

Phone Number:

E-mail:

Make as many copies of this form as needed.

Name:

Address:

City:

State: Zip Code:

Phone Number:

E-mail:

Name:

Address:

City:

State: Zip Code:

Phone Number:

E-mail:

Name:

Address:

City:

State: Zip Code:

Phone Number:

E-mail:

Name:

Address:

City:

State: Zip Code:

Phone Number:

E-mail:

Name:

Address:

City:

State: Zip Code:

Phone Number:

E-mail:

Name:

Address:

City:

State: Zip Code:

Phone Number:

E-mail:

Name:

Address:

City:

State: Zip Code:

Phone Number:

E-mail:

Name:

Address:

City:

State: Zip Code:

Phone Number:

E-mail:

Name:

Address:

City:

State: Zip Code:

Phone Number:

E-mail:

Name:

Address:

City:

State: Zip Code:

Phone Number:

E-mail:

ANNOUNCEMENT LIST

Make as many copies of this form as needed.

Name:

Address:

City:

State: Zip Code:

Phone Number:

E-mail:

Name:

Address:

City:

State: Zip Code:

Phone Number:

E-mail:

Name:

Address:

City:

State: Zip Code:

Phone Number:

E-mail:

Name:

Address:

City:

State: Zip Code:

Phone Number:

E-mail:

Name:

Address:

City:

State: Zip Code:

Phone Number:

E-mail:

Name:

Address:

City:

State: Zip Code:

Phone Number:

E-mail:

Name:

Address:

City:

State: Zip Code:

Phone Number:

E-mail:

Name:

Address:

City:

State: Zip Code:

Phone Number:

E-mail:

Name:

Address:

City:

State: Zip Code:

Phone Number:

E-mail:

Name:

Address:

City:

State: Zip Code:

Phone Number:

E-mail:

ANNOUNCEMENT LIST

Make as many copies of this form as needed.

Name:

Address:

City:

State: Zip Code:

Phone Number:

E-mail:

Name:

Address:

City:

State: Zip Code:

Phone Number:

E-mail:

Name:

Address:

City:

State: Zip Code:

Phone Number:

E-mail:

Name:

Address:

City:

State: Zip Code:

Phone Number:

E-mail:

Name:

Address:

City:

State: Zip Code:

Phone Number:

E-mail:

Name:

Address:

City:

State: Zip Code:

Phone Number:

E-mail:

Name:

Address:

City:

State: Zip Code:

Phone Number:

E-mail:

Name:

Address:

City:

State: Zip Code:

Phone Number:

E-mail:

Name:

Address:

City:

State: Zip Code:

Phone Number:

E-mail:

Name:

Address:

City:

State: Zip Code:

Phone Number:

E-mail:

GUEST ACCOMMODATION LIST

Make as many copies of this form as needed.

Name: _____

Arrival Date: _____ Time: _____

Airline/Train: _____

Flight/Train No. _____

Pick Up By: _____

Will Stay At: _____

Address: _____

City: _____

State: _____ Zip Code: _____

Phone Number: _____

Cost Per Room: _____

Confirmation No. _____

Departure Date: _____ Time: _____

Taken By: _____

Airline/Train: _____

Flight/Train No. _____

Name: _____

Arrival Date: _____ Time: _____

Airline/Train: _____

Flight/Train No. _____

Pick Up By: _____

Will Stay At: _____

Address: _____

City: _____

State: _____ Zip Code: _____

Phone Number: _____

Cost Per Room: _____

Confirmation No. _____

Departure Date: _____ Time: _____

Taken By: _____

Airline/Train: _____

Flight/Train No. _____

Name: _____

Arrival Date: _____ Time: _____

Airline/Train: _____

Flight/Train No. _____

Pick Up By: _____

Will Stay At: _____

Address: _____

City: _____

State: _____ Zip Code: _____

Phone Number: _____

Cost Per Room: _____

Confirmation No. _____

Departure Date: _____ Time: _____

Taken By: _____

Airline/Train: _____

Flight/Train No. _____

Name: _____

Arrival Date: _____ Time: _____

Airline/Train: _____

Flight/Train No. _____

Pick Up By: _____

Will Stay At: _____

Address: _____

City: _____

State: _____ Zip Code: _____

Phone Number: _____

Cost Per Room: _____

Confirmation No. _____

Departure Date: _____ Time: _____

Taken By: _____

Airline/Train: _____

Flight/Train No. _____

GUEST ACCOMMODATION LIST

Make as many copies of this form as needed.

Name:

Arrival Date:	Time:
Airline/Train:	
Flight/Train No.	
Pick Up By:	
Will Stay At:	
Address:	
City:	

State:	Zip Code:
Phone Number:	
Cost Per Room:	
Confirmation No.	
Departure Date:	Time:
Taken By:	
Airline/Train:	
Flight/Train No.	

Name:

Arrival Date:	Time:
Airline/Train:	
Flight/Train No.	
Pick Up By:	
Will Stay At:	
Address:	
City:	

State:	Zip Code:
Phone Number:	
Cost Per Room:	
Confirmation No.	
Departure Date:	Time:
Taken By:	
Airline/Train:	
Flight/Train No.	

Name:

Arrival Date:	Time:
Airline/Train:	
Flight/Train No.	
Pick Up By:	
Will Stay At:	
Address:	
City:	

State:	Zip Code:
Phone Number:	
Cost Per Room:	
Confirmation No.	
Departure Date:	Time:
Taken By:	
Airline/Train:	
Flight/Train No.	

Name:

Arrival Date:	Time:
Airline/Train:	
Flight/Train No.	
Pick Up By:	
Will Stay At:	
Address:	
City:	

State:	Zip Code:
Phone Number:	
Cost Per Room:	
Confirmation No.	
Departure Date:	Time:
Taken By:	
Airline/Train:	
Flight/Train No.	

GUEST ACCOMMODATION LIST

Make as many copies of this form as needed.

Name: _____ State: _____ Zip Code: _____
Arrival Date: _____ Time: _____ Phone Number: _____
Airline/Train: _____ Cost Per Room: _____
Flight/Train No. _____ Confirmation No. _____
Pick Up By: _____ Departure Date: _____ Time: _____
Will Stay At: _____ Taken By: _____
Address: _____ Airline/Train: _____
City: _____ Flight/Train No. _____

Name: _____ State: _____ Zip Code: _____
Arrival Date: _____ Time: _____ Phone Number: _____
Airline/Train: _____ Cost Per Room: _____
Flight/Train No. _____ Confirmation No. _____
Pick Up By: _____ Departure Date: _____ Time: _____
Will Stay At: _____ Taken By: _____
Address: _____ Airline/Train: _____
City: _____ Flight/Train No. _____

Name: _____ State: _____ Zip Code: _____
Arrival Date: _____ Time: _____ Phone Number: _____
Airline/Train: _____ Cost Per Room: _____
Flight/Train No. _____ Confirmation No. _____
Pick Up By: _____ Departure Date: _____ Time: _____
Will Stay At: _____ Taken By: _____
Address: _____ Airline/Train: _____
City: _____ Flight/Train No. _____

Name: _____ State: _____ Zip Code: _____
Arrival Date: _____ Time: _____ Phone Number: _____
Airline/Train: _____ Cost Per Room: _____
Flight/Train No. _____ Confirmation No. _____
Pick Up By: _____ Departure Date: _____ Time: _____
Will Stay At: _____ Taken By: _____
Address: _____ Airline/Train: _____
City: _____ Flight/Train No. _____

GUEST ACCOMMODATION LIST

Make as many copies of this form as needed.

Name:

Arrival Date: Time:

Airline/Train:

Flight/Train No.

Pick Up By:

Will Stay At:

Address:

City:

State: Zip Code:

Phone Number:

Cost Per Room:

Confirmation No.

Departure Date: Time:

Taken By:

Airline/Train:

Flight/Train No.

Name:

Arrival Date: Time:

Airline/Train:

Flight/Train No.

Pick Up By:

Will Stay At:

Address:

City:

State: Zip Code:

Phone Number:

Cost Per Room:

Confirmation No.

Departure Date: Time:

Taken By:

Airline/Train:

Flight/Train No.

Name:

Arrival Date: Time:

Airline/Train:

Flight/Train No.

Pick Up By:

Will Stay At:

Address:

City:

State: Zip Code:

Phone Number:

Cost Per Room:

Confirmation No.

Departure Date: Time:

Taken By:

Airline/Train:

Flight/Train No.

Name:

Arrival Date: Time:

Airline/Train:

Flight/Train No.

Pick Up By:

Will Stay At:

Address:

City:

State: Zip Code:

Phone Number:

Cost Per Room:

Confirmation No.

Departure Date: Time:

Taken By:

Airline/Train:

Flight/Train No.

RECEIVING LINE

An example of a traditional receiving line is found on page 244. To design yours, simply place the names of the people you want to include and the order in which you want them to stand.

When: _____ Where: _____

TRADITIONAL RECEIVING LINE: **YOUR RECEIVING LINE:**

Mother of the Bride   _____

Father of the Bride (optional)   _____

Mother of the Groom   _____

Father of the Groom (optional)   _____

Bride   _____

Groom   _____

Maid of Honor   _____

Best Man   _____

Regardless of how you structure your receiving line, the mother of the bride should always be first.

Close family members, bridesmaids, and ushers can also be included in the receiving line, if you wish.

Please note that for a large wedding (over 100 guests) we do not recommend a receiving line because it takes too long for your guests to go through it.

ADDRESSING
INVITATIONS

GUIDELINES FOR ADDRESSING INVITATIONS: We recommend that you start addressing your envelopes at least three months before your wedding, preferably four months if you are using calligraphy or if your guest list is above 200. You may want to ask your maid of honor or bridesmaids to help you with this time-consuming task, as this is traditionally part of their responsibilities. Organize a luncheon or late afternoon get-together with hors d'oeuvres and make a party out of it! If you are working with a wedding consultant, s/he can also help you address invitations.

There are typically two envelopes that need to be addressed for wedding invitations: an inner envelope and an outer envelope. The inner envelope is placed unsealed inside the outer envelope, with the flap away from the person inserting it.

The invitation and all enclosures are placed inside the inner envelope facing the back flap. The inner envelope contains the name (or names) of the person (or people) who are invited to the ceremony and/or reception. The address is not included on the inner envelope.

The outer envelope contains the name (or names) and address of the person (or people) to whom the inner envelope belongs.

Use the guidelines on the following page to help you properly address both the inner and outer envelopes.

ADDRESSING INVITATIONS

SITUATION	INNER ENVELOPE	OUTER ENVELOPE
	No first name or address	Has first name & address
HUSBAND AND WIFE (WITH SAME SURNAME)	MR. AND MRS. SMITH	MR. AND MRS. THOMAS SMITH (USE MIDDLE NAME, IF KNOWN)
HUSBAND AND WIFE (WITH DIFFERENT SURNAMES)	MS. BANKS AND MR. SMITH (WIFE FIRST)	MS. ANITA BANKS MR. THOMAS SMITH (WIFE'S NAME & TITLE ABOVE HUSBAND'S)
HUSBAND AND WIFE (WIFE HAS PROFESSIONAL TITLE)	DR. SMITH AND MR. SMITH	DR. ANITA SMITH MR. THOMAS SMITH (WIFE'S NAME & TITLE ABOVE HUSBAND'S)
HUSBAND AND WIFE (WITH CHILDREN UNDER 16)	MR. AND MRS. SMITH JOHN, MARY, AND GLEN (IN ORDER OF AGE)	MR. AND MRS. THOMAS SMITH
SINGLE WOMAN (REGARDLESS OF AGE)	MISS/MS. SMITH	MISS/MS. BEVERLY SMITH
SINGLE WOMAN AND GUEST	MISS/MS. SMITH MR. JONES (OR "AND GUEST")	MISS/MS. BEVERLY SMITH
SINGLE MAN	MR. JONES (MASTER FOR A YOUNG BOY)	MR. WILLIAM JONES
SINGLE MAN AND GUEST	MR. JONES MISS/MS. SMITH (OR "AND GUEST")	MR. WILLIAM JONES
UNMARRIED COUPLE LIVING TOGETHER	MR. KNIGHT AND MS. ORLANDI (NAMES LISTED ALPHABETICALLY)	MR. MICHAEL KNIGHT MS. PAULA ORLANDI
TWO SISTERS (OVER 16)	THE MISSES SMITH	THE MISSES MARY AND JANE SMITH (IN ORDER OF AGE)
TWO BROTHERS (OVER 16)	THE MESSRS. SMITH	THE MESSRS. JOHN AND GLEN SMITH (IN ORDER OF AGE)
BROTHERS & SISTERS (OVER 16)	MARY, JANE, JOHN & GLEN (NAME THE GIRLS FIRST, IN ORDER OF AGE)	THE MISSES SMITH THE MESSRS. SMITH (NAME THE GIRLS FIRST)
A BROTHER AND SISTER (OVER 16)	JANE AND JOHN (NAME THE GIRL FIRST)	MISS JANE SMITH AND MR. JOHN SMITH (NAME THE GIRL FIRST)
WIDOW	MRS. SMITH	MRS. WILLIAM SMITH
DIVORCEE	MRS. SMITH	MRS. JONES SMITH (MAIDEN NAME AND FORMER HUSBAND'S SURNAME)

RECEPTION

THE RECEPTION IS A PARTY WHERE ALL YOUR GUESTS come together to celebrate your new life as a married couple. It should reflect and complement the formality of your ceremony. The selection of a reception site will depend on its availability, price, proximity to the ceremony site, and the number of people it will accommodate.

RECEPTION SITE FEE

There are two basic types of reception sites. The first type charges a per person fee which includes the facility, food, tables, silverware, china, and so forth. Examples: hotels, restaurants and catered yachts. The second type charges a room rental fee and you are responsible for providing the food, beverages, linens, and possibly tables and chairs. Examples: clubs, halls, parks, museums, and private homes.

The advantage of the first type is that most everything is done for you. The disadvantage, however, is that your choices of food, china, and linen are limited. Usually you are not permitted to bring in an outside caterer and must select from a predetermined menu.

Options: Private homes, gardens, hotels, clubs, restaurants, halls, parks, museums, yachts, and wineries are some of the more popular choices for receptions.

Things to Consider: When comparing the cost of different locations, consider the rental fee, food, beverages, parking, gratuity, set-up charges, and the cost of rental equipment needed such as tables, chairs, canopies, and so forth. If you are planning an outdoor reception, be sure to have a backup site in case of rain.

Beware: Some hotels are known for double booking. A bride may reserve the largest or most elegant room in a hotel for her reception, only to find out later that the hotel took the liberty to book a more profitable event in the room she had reserved and moved her reception over to a smaller or less elegant room.

Also be careful of hotels that book events too close together. You don't want your guests to wait outside while your room is being set up for the reception. And you don't want to be "forced out" before you are ready to leave because the hotel needs to arrange the room for the next reception. Get your rental hours and the name of your room in writing.

Tips to Save Money: Since the cost of the reception is approximately 35 percent of the total cost of your wedding, you can save the most money by limiting your guest list. If you hire a wedding consultant, s/he may be able to cut your cake and save you the cake-cutting fee. Check this out with your facility or caterer. Reception sites that charge a room rental fee may waive this fee if you meet minimum requirements on food and beverages consumed. Try to negotiate this before you book the facility.

Price Range: $300 - $5,000

HORS D' OEUVRES

At receptions where a full meal is to be served, hors d' oeuvres may be offered to guests during the first hour of the reception. However, at a tea or cocktail reception, hors d' oeuvres will be the "main course."

Options: There are many options for hors d' oeuvres, depending on the formality of your reception and the type of food to be served at the meal. Popular items are foods that can easily be picked up and eaten with one hand. Hors d' oeuvres may be set out on tables "buffet style" for guests to help themselves, or they may be passed around on trays by waiters and waitresses.

Things to Consider: When selecting hors d' oeuvres for your reception, consider whether heating or refrigeration will be available and choose your food accordingly. When planning your menu, consider the time of day. You should select lighter hors d' oeuvres for a midday reception and heavier hors d' oeuvres for an evening reception.

Tips to Save Money: Tray pass hors d' oeuvres during cocktail hour and serve a lighter meal. Avoid serving hors d' oeuvres that are labor intensive or that require expensive ingredients. Compare two or three caterers; there is a wide price range between caterers for the same food. Compare the total cost of catering (main entree plus hors d' oeuvres) when selecting a caterer. Consider serving hors d' oeuvres "buffet style." Your guests will eat less this way than if waiters and waitresses are constantly serving them hors d' oeuvres.

Price Range: $3.00 - $20 per person

MAIN MEAL/CATERER

If your reception is going to be at a hotel, restaurant, or other facility that provides food, you will need to select a meal to serve your guests. Most of these facilities will have a predetermined menu from which to select your meal. If your reception is going to be in a facility that does not provide food, you will need to hire an outside caterer. The caterer will be responsible for preparing, cooking, and serving the food. The caterer will also be responsible for beverages and for cleaning up after the event. Before signing a contract, make sure you understand all the services the caterer will provide. Your contract should state the amount and type of food and beverages that will be served, the way in which they will be served, the number of servers who will be available, and the cost per food item or person and the rental items the caterer will provide such as tables, chairs, and tableware.

Options: Food can be served either buffet style or as a sit-down meal. It should be chosen according to the time of day, year, and formality of the wedding. Although there are many main dishes to choose from, chicken and beef are the most popular selections for a large event. Ask your facility manager or caterer for their specialty. If you have a special type of food you would like to serve at your reception, select a facility or caterer who specializes in preparing it.

Things to Consider: When hiring a caterer, check to see if the location of your reception provides refrigeration and cooking equipment. If not, make sure your caterer is fully self-supported with portable refrigeration and heating equipment. A competent caterer will prepare much of the food in his/her own kitchen and should provide an adequate staff of cooks, servers, and bartenders. Ask for references and look at photos from previous parties so you know how the food will be presented; or better yet, visit an event they are catering.

Beware: Avoid mayonnaise, cream sauces, or custard fillings if food must go unrefrigerated for any length of time.

Tips to Save Money: Give only 85 to 95 percent of your final guest count to your caterer or facility manager, depending on how certain you are that all of your guests who have responded will come. Chances are that several, if not many, of your guests will not show up. But if they do, your caterer should have enough food for all of them. This is especially true with buffet style receptions, in which case the facility or caterer will charge extra for each additional guest. However, if you give a complete count of your guests to your caterer and some of them don't show up, you will still have to pay for their plates. If offering a buffet meal, have the catering staff serve the food onto guests' plates rather than allowing guests to serve themselves. This will help to regulate the amount of food consumed.

Select food that is not too time-consuming to prepare, or food that does not have expensive ingredients. Also, consider a brunch or early afternoon wedding so the reception will fall between meals, allowing you to serve hors d' oeuvres instead of a full meal. Or tray pass hors d' oeuvres during cocktail hour and choose a lighter meal.

Price Range: $20 - $100 per person

RECEPTION

LIQUOR/BEVERAGES

Prices for liquor and beverages vary greatly, depending on the amount and brand of alcohol served. Traditionally, at least champagne or punch should be served to toast the couple.

Options: White and red wines, scotch, vodka, gin, rum, and beer are the most popular alcoholic beverages. Sodas and fruit punch are popular nonalcoholic beverages served at receptions. And of course, don't forget coffee or tea. There are a number of options and variations for serving alcoholic beverages: a full, open bar where you pay for your guests to drink as much as they wish; an open bar for the first hour, followed by a cash bar where guests pay for their own drinks; cash bar only; beer and wine only; nonalcoholic beverages only; or any combination thereof.

Things to Consider: If you plan to serve alcoholic beverages at a reception site that does not provide liquor, make sure your caterer has a license to serve alcohol and that your reception site allows alcoholic beverages. If you plan to order your own alcohol, do so three or four weeks before the event. If you plan to have a no-host or "cash" bar, consider notifying your guests so they know to bring cash with them. A simple line that says "No-Host Bar" on the reception card should suffice.

In selecting the type of alcohol to serve, consider the age and preference of your guests, the type of food that will be served, and the time of day your guests will be drinking.

On the average, you should allow one drink per person per hour at the reception. A bottle of champagne will usually serve six glasses. Never serve liquor without some type of food. Use the following chart to plan your beverage needs:

Beverages	Amount based on 100 guests
Bourbon	3 Fifths
Gin	3 Fifths
Rum	2 Fifths
Scotch	4 Quarts
Vodka	5 Quarts
White Wine	2 Cases
Red Wine	1 Case
Champagne	3 Cases
Other	2 Cases each: Club Soda, Seltzer Water, Tonic Water, Ginger Ale, Cola, Beer

If you are hosting an open bar at a hotel or restaurant, ask the catering manager how they charge for liquor: by consumption or by number of bottles opened. Get this in writing before the event and then ask for a full consumption report after the event.

Beware: In today's society, it is not uncommon for the hosts of a party to be held legally responsible for the conduct and safety of their guests. Keep this in mind when planning the quantity and type of beverages to serve. Also, be sure to remind your bartenders not to serve alcohol to minors.

Tips to Save Money: To keep beverage costs down, serve punch, wine, or nonalcoholic drinks only. If your caterer allows it, consider buying liquor from a wholesaler who will let you return unopened bottles. Also, avoid salty foods such as potato chips, pretzels, or ham. These foods will make your guests thirstier so they will tend to drink more.

Host alcoholic beverages for the first hour, then go to a cash bar. You can also choose to host beer, wine, and soft drinks only and have mixed drinks available on a cash basis. The bartending fee is often waived if you meet the minimum requirements on beverages consumed. For the toast, tray pass champagne only to those guests who want it, not to everyone. Many people will make a toast with whatever they are currently drinking. Consider serving sparkling cider in place of champagne.

Omit waiters and waitresses. Instead, have an open bar in which your guests have to get their own drinks. People tend to drink almost twice as much if there are waiters and waitresses constantly asking them if they would like another drink and then bringing drinks to them.

Price Range: $8.00 - $35 per person

BARTENDING/BAR SET-UP FEE

Some reception sites and caterers charge an extra fee for bartending and for setting up the bar.

Tips to Save Money: The bartending fee could be and often is waived if you meet a minimum requirement on beverages consumed. Try to negotiate this with your caterer prior to hiring him/her.

Price Range: $75 - $500

RECEPTION

CORKAGE FEE

Many reception sites and caterers make money by marking up the food and alcohol they sell. You may wish to provide your own alcohol for several reasons. First, it is more cost effective. Second, you may want to serve an exotic wine or champagne that the reception site or caterer does not offer. In either case, and if your reception site or caterer allows it, be prepared to pay a corkage fee. This is the fee for each bottle brought into the reception site and opened by a member of their staff.

Things to Consider: You need to consider whether the expenses saved after paying the corkage fee justify the hassle and liability of bringing in your own alcohol.

Price Range: $5.00 - $20/bottle

FEE TO POUR COFFEE

In addition to corkage and cake-cutting fees, some facilities also charge extra to pour coffee with the wedding cake.

Things to Consider: Again, when comparing the cost of various reception sites, don't forget to add up all the extra miscellaneous costs, such as the fee for pouring coffee.

Price Range: $0.25 - $1.00 per person

SERVICE PROVIDERS' MEALS

Things to Consider: It is considered a courtesy to feed your photographer, videographer, and any other "service provider" at the reception. Check options and prices with your caterer or reception site manager. Make sure you allocate a place for your service providers to eat. You may want them to eat with your guests, or you may prefer setting a place outside the main room for them to eat. Your service providers may be more comfortable with the latter.

Tips to Save Money: You don't need to feed your service providers the same meal as your guests. You can order sandwiches or another less expensive meal for them. If the meal is a buffet, there should be enough food left after all your guests have been served for your service providers to eat. Tell them they are welcome to eat after all your guests have been served. Be sure to discuss this with your catering manager.

Price Range: $10 - $30 per person

GRATUITY

It is customary to pay a gratuity fee to your caterer. The average gratuity is 15% to 20% of your food and beverage bill.

Tips to Save Money: Gratuities can range from 15% to 25%. Ask about these costs up front and select your caterer or reception site accordingly.

Price Range: 15% - 25%

PARTY FAVORS

Party favors are little gift items given to your guests as mementos of your wedding. They add a very special touch to your wedding and can become keepsakes for your guests.

Options: White matchboxes engraved with the couple's names and wedding date, cocktail napkins marked in the same way, individually wrapped and marked chocolates, almonds, or fine candy are all popular party favors. Wine or champagne bottles marked with the bride and groom's names and wedding date on a personalized label are also very popular. These come in different sizes and can be purchased by the case.

If you can afford it, you may also consider porcelain or ceramic party favors. These can be custom-fired with your name and wedding date on them. A new idea that's gaining in popularity among environmentally conscientious couples is to present each guest with a tiny shoot of an endangered tree to be planted in honor of the bride and groom.

Things to Consider: Personalized favors need to be ordered several weeks in advance.

Price Range: $1.00 - $25/favor

DISPOSABLE CAMERAS

A great way to inexpensively obtain many candid photographs of your wedding day is to place a disposable 35 mm camera loaded with film on each table at your reception and to have your guests take shots of the event! Disposable cameras come pre-loaded with film. Your guests can leave the cameras at their table or drop them in a basket or other labeled container near the entrance to the reception site. Arrange for someone to collect the cameras after the event. Tell your DJ, musician, or wedding coordinator to encourage your guests to take photographs with the disposables. You will end up with many beautiful, memorable, and candid photographs of your reception.

Things to Consider: Disposable cameras are sold with or without flash. Disposable cameras with flash are more expensive but necessary if your reception is going to be held indoors or in the evening. If you are planning a large reception, consider buying cameras with only 12 exposures. Otherwise, you may end up with too many photographs. For example, if 200 guests attend your reception and you seat 8 guests per table, you will need to purchase 25 cameras. If each camera has 36 exposures, you will end up with 825 photographs. If the cameras have only 12 exposures, you will end up with 300 photographs, which is a much more reasonable quantity!

Tips to Save Money: Instead of developing these photographs into print and then placing them into a big album, have your videographer transfer the negatives directly onto video set to your favorite music. You can then reproduce this "photo montage" and send it as a gift to your friends and family members. You can later decide which of these photographs you want to develop into print.

Price Range: $4.00 - $20/camera

ROSE PETALS/RICE

Rose petals or rice are traditionally tossed over the bride and groom as they leave the church after the ceremony or when they leave the reception. These are usually handed out to guests in little sachet bags while the bride and groom are changing into their going away clothes. This tradition was initiated in the Middle Ages whereby a handful of wheat was thrown over the bridal couple as a symbol of fertility. Rose petals are used to symbolize happiness, beauty, and prosperity.

Options: Rose petals, rice, or confetti is often used. However, an environmentally correct alternative is to use grass or flower seeds, which do not need to be "cleaned up" if tossed over a grassy area. These come wrapped in attractive, recycled packages with the couple's names and wedding date printed on the front.

Things to Consider: Rose petals can stain carpets; rice can sting faces, harm birds, and make stairs dangerously slippery; confetti is messy and hard to clean. Clubs and hotels seldom permit the use of any of these. Ask about their policy.

Price Range: $0.35 - $2.00 per person

GIFT ATTENDANT

The gift attendant is responsible for watching over your gifts during the reception so that no one walks away with them. This is necessary only if your reception is held in a public area such as a hotel or outside garden where strangers may be walking by. It is not proper to have a friend or family member take on this duty as s/he would not enjoy the reception. The gift attendant should also be responsible for transporting your gifts from the reception site to your car or bridal suite.

Tips to Save Money: Hire a young boy or girl from your neighborhood to watch over your gifts at the reception.

Price Range: $20 - $100

PARKING FEE/VALET SERVICES

Many reception sites such as hotels, restaurants, etc. charge for parking. It is customary, although not necessary, for the host of the wedding to pay this charge. At a large home reception, you should consider hiring a professional, qualified valet service if parking could be a problem. If so, make sure the valet service is fully insured.

Things to Consider: When comparing the cost of reception sites, don't forget to add the cost of parking to the total price.

Tips to Save Money: To save money, let your guests pay their own parking fees.

Price Range: $3.00 - $10/car

RECEPTION SITE COMPARISON CHART

QUESTIONS	POSSIBILITY 1
What is the name of the reception site?	
What is the website and e-mail of the reception site?	
What is the address of the reception site?	
What is the name and phone number of my contact person?	
What dates are available?	
What times are available?	
What is the maximum number of guests for a seated reception?	
What is the maximum number of guests for a cocktail reception?	
What is the reception site fee?	
What is the price range for a seated lunch? What is the price range for a buffet lunch?	
What is the price range for a seated dinner? What is the price range for a buffet dinner?	
What is the corkage fee?	
What is the cake-cutting fee?	
What is the ratio of servers to guests?	
How much time will be allotted for my reception?	
What music restrictions are there, if any?	
What alcohol restrictions are there, if any?	

RECEPTION SITE COMPARISON CHART

POSSIBILITY 2	POSSIBILITY 3

RECEPTION SITE COMPARISON CHART

QUESTIONS	POSSIBILITY 1
Are there any restrictions for rice or rose petal-tossing?	
What room and table decorations are available?	
Is a changing room available?	
Is there handicap accessibility?	
Is a dance floor included in the site fee?	
Are tables, chairs, and linens included in the site fee?	
Are outside caterers allowed?	
Are kitchen facilities available for outside caterers?	
Does the facility have full liability insurance?	
What "perks" or giveaways are offered?	
How many parking spaces are available for my wedding party?	
How many parking spaces are available for my guests?	
What is the cost for parking, if any?	
What is the cost for sleeping rooms, if available?	
What is the payment policy?	
What is the cancellation policy?	

RECEPTION SITE COMPARISON CHART

POSSIBILITY 2	POSSIBILITY 3

RECEPTION SITE INFORMATION SHEET

RECEPTION SITE

Location Name:

Site Coordinator: Cost:

Website:

E-mail:

Phone Number: Fax Number:

Address:

City: State: Zip Code:

Name of Room: Room Capacity:

Date Confirmed: Confirm Head-Count By:

Beginning Time: Ending Time:

Cocktails/Hors d'oeuvres Time: Meal Time:

Color of Linens: Color of Napkins:

TOTAL COST: Deposit: Date:

Balance: Date Due:

Cancellation Policy:

EQUIPMENT INCLUDES:

❑ Tables   ❑ Chairs   ❑ Linens   ❑ Tableware

❑ Barware   ❑ Heaters   ❑ Electric Outlet   ❑ Musical Instruments

SERVICE INCLUDES:

❑ Waiters   ❑ Bartenders   ❑ Valet   ❑ Main Meal

❑ Cleanup   ❑ Set-up   ❑ Security   ❑ Free Parking

CATERER INFORMATION SHEET

CATERER

Business Name:

Contact Person: Cost Per Person:

Website:

E-mail:

Phone Number: Fax Number:

Address:

City: State: Zip Code:

Confirmed Date: Confirm Head-Count By:

Arrival Time: Departure Time:

Cocktails/Hors d'oeuvres Time: Meal Time:

Color of Linens: Color of Napkins:

TOTAL COST: Deposit: Date:

Balance: Date Due:

Cancellation Policy:

EQUIPMENT INCLUDES:

❑ Tables   ❑ Chairs   ❑ Linens   ❑ Tableware

❑ Barware   ❑ Heaters   ❑ Lighting   ❑ Candles

SERVICE INCLUDES:

❑ Waiters   ❑ Bartenders   ❑ Set-up   ❑ Clean-up

❑ Security   ❑ Hors d'oeuvres   ❑ Buffet Meal   ❑ Seated Meal

❑ Cocktails   ❑ Champagne   ❑ Wine   ❑ Beer

❑ Punch   ❑ Soft Drinks   ❑ Coffee/Tea   ❑ Cake

TABLE SEATING ARRANGEMENTS

Complete this form only after finalizing your guest list.
Make as many copies of this form as needed.

• HEAD TABLE

_____
_____
_____
_____
_____
_____
_____

• BRIDE'S FAMILY TABLE

_____
_____
_____
_____
_____
_____
_____

•GROOM'S FAMILY TABLE

_____
_____
_____
_____
_____
_____
_____

• TABLE __

_____
_____
_____
_____
_____
_____
_____

• TABLE __

_____
_____
_____
_____
_____
_____
_____

• TABLE __

_____
_____
_____
_____
_____
_____
_____

• TABLE __

_____
_____
_____
_____
_____
_____
_____

• TABLE __

_____
_____
_____
_____
_____
_____
_____

TABLE SEATING ARRANGEMENTS

Complete this form only after finalizing your guest list.
Make as many copies of this form as needed.

• **TABLE __**

• **TABLE __**

• **TABLE __**

• **TABLE __**

• **TABLE __**

• **TABLE __**

• **TABLE __**

• **TABLE __**

LIQUOR ORDER FORM

LIQUOR STORE:

Date Ordered:

Salesperson: Phone Number:

Website:

E-mail:

Address:

City: State: Zip Code:

Cost:

Delivered by: Delivery Date:

TYPE OF LIQUOR	# of Bottles Needed	Price

PARTY FAVORS COMPARISON CHART

White matchboxes engraved with names of bride and groom and date of the wedding

Company:

Website:

Qty: _____ Price:

Cocktail napkins engraved with names of the bride and groom and date of the wedding

Company:

Website:

Qty: _____ Price:

Almonds, chocolates, or other fine candy

Company:

Website:

Qty: _____ Price:

Favor Description:

Company:

Website:

Qty: _____ Price:

Favor Description:

Company:

Website:

Qty: _____ Price:

Favor Description:

Company:

Website:

Qty: _____ Price:

CATERER COMPARISON CHART

QUESTIONS	POSSIBILITY 1
What is the name of the caterer?	
What is the website and e-mail of the caterer?	
What is the address of the caterer?	
What is the name and phone number of my contact person?	
How many years have you been in business?	
What percentage of your business is dedicated to receptions?	
Do you have liability insurance/license to serve alcohol?	
When is the final head-count needed?	
What is your ratio of servers to guests?	
How do your servers dress for wedding receptions?	
What is your price range for a seated lunch/buffet lunch?	
What is your price range for a seated dinner/buffet dinner?	
How much gratuity is expected?	
What is your specialty?	
What is your cake-cutting fee? What is your bartending fee?	
What is your fee to clean-up after the reception?	
What is your payment/cancellation policy?	

CATERER COMPARISON CHART

POSSIBILITY 2	POSSIBILITY 3

MENU WORKSHEET

HORS D'OEUVRES:

SALADS/APPETIZERS:

SOUPS:

MAIN ENTREE:

DESSERTS:

WEDDING CAKE:

MUSIC

CEREMONY MUSIC INCLUDES THE MUSIC PLAYED DURING the prelude, processional, ceremony, recessional, and postlude. Prelude music is played 15 to 30 minutes before the ceremony begins and while guests are being seated. Processional music is played as the wedding party enters the ceremony site. Recessional music is played as the wedding party leaves the ceremony site. Postlude music is played while the guests leave the ceremony site.

CEREMONY MUSIC

Options: The most traditional musical instrument for wedding ceremonies is the organ. But guitars, pianos, flutes, harps, and violins are also popular today.

Popular selections for a Christian wedding:

"Trumpet Voluntary" by Purcell
"The Bridal Chorus" by Wagner
"Wedding March" by Mendelssohn
"Postlude in G Major" by Handel
"Canon in D Major" by Pachelbel
"Adagio in A Minor" by Bach

Popular selections for a Jewish wedding:

"Erev Shel Shoshanim"
"Erev Ba"
"Hana' Ava Babanot"

Things to Consider: Music may or may not be included as part of the ceremony site fee. Be sure to check with your ceremony site about restrictions pertaining to music and the availability of musical instruments for your use. Discuss the selection of ceremony music with your officiant and musicians. Make sure the musicians know how to play the selections you request.

When selecting ceremony music, keep in mind the formality of your wedding, your religious affiliation, and the length of the ceremony. Also consider the location and time of day. If the ceremony is outside where there may be other noises such as traffic, wind, or people's voices, or if a large number of guests will be attending your ceremony, consider having the music, your officiant, and your vows amplified. Make sure there are electrical outlets close to where the instruments will be set up.

Tips to Save Money: Hire student musicians from your local university or high school. Ask a friend to sing or play at your ceremony; they will be honored. If you're planning to hire a band for your reception, consider hiring a scaled-down version of the same band to play at your ceremony, such as a trio of flute, guitar, and vocals. This could enable you to negotiate a "package" price. If you're planning to hire a DJ for your reception, consider hiring him/her to play pre-recorded music at your ceremony.

Price Range: **$100 - $900**

RECEPTION MUSIC

Music is a major part of your reception and should be planned carefully. Music helps create the atmosphere of your wedding. Special songs will make your reception unique. When you select music for your reception, keep in mind the age and musical preference of your guests, your budget, and any restrictions that the reception site may have. Bands and musicians are typically more expensive than DJ's.

Options: There are many options for reception music. You can hire a DJ, a band, an orchestra, or any combination of one or more instruments and vocalists.

Things to Consider: Consider hiring an entertainment agency that can help you choose a reliable DJ or band that will play the type of music you want. Whoever you choose should have experience performing at wedding receptions.

If you want your musician to act as a master of ceremonies, make sure s/he has a complete timeline for your reception in order to announce the various events such as the toasts, first dance, and cutting of the cake. Consider watching your musicians perform at another event before booking their services.

If you need a large variety of music to satisfy all your guests, consider hiring a DJ. A professional DJ can play any type of music and may even offer a light show. Make sure you give him/her a list of the songs you want played at your reception and the sequence in which you want them played. Make sure there are electrical outlets at the reception site close to where the musicians will be performing.

Tips to Save Money: You will probably get a better price if you hire a band or DJ directly than if you hire them through an entertainment agency. Check the music department of local colleges and universities for names of student musicians and DJs. You may be able to hire a student for a fraction of the price of a professional musician or DJ. A DJ is typically less expensive than a "live" musician, saving $200 - $1,000.

Some facilities have contracts with certain DJ's, and you may be able to save money by hiring one of them.

Price Range: **$500 - $5,000**

Bonus Tip: For suggestions on appropriate music for each moment of the wedding, you should consider purchasing *The Ultimate Guide to Wedding Music*. This guide is published by Wedding Solutions and is available at most major bookstores. It contains lyrics for 100 of the most popular love songs for weddings. It also includes an audio CD with excerpts from 99 of the most popular classical music pieces for weddings.

CEREMONY MUSIC COMPARISON CHART

QUESTIONS	POSSIBILITY 1
What is the name of the musician or band?	
What is the website and e-mail of the musician or band?	
What is the address of the musician or band?	
What is the name and phone number of my contact person?	
How many years of professional experience do you have?	
What percentage of your business is dedicated to weddings?	
Are you the person who will perform at my wedding?	
What instrument(s) do you play?	
What type of music do you specialize in?	
What are your hourly fees?	
What is the cost of a soloist?	
What is the cost of a duet?	
What is the cost of a trio?	
What is the cost of a quartet?	
How would you dress for my wedding?	
Do you have a cordless microphone?	
Do you have liability insurance? What is your payment/cancellation policy?	

CEREMONY MUSIC COMPARISON CHART

POSSIBILITY 2	POSSIBILITY 3

RECEPTION MUSIC COMPARISON CHART

QUESTIONS	POSSIBILITY 1
What is the name of the musician? Band? DJ?	
What is the website and e-mail of the musician? Band? DJ?	
What is the address of the musician? Band? DJ?	
What is the name and phone number of my contact person?	
How many years of professional experience do you have?	
What percentage of your business is dedicated to receptions?	
How many people are in your band?	
What type of music do you specialize in?	
What type of sound system do you have?	
Can you act as a master of ceremonies?	
How do you dress for receptions?	
Do you have a cordless microphone?	
How many breaks do you take? How long are they?	
Do you play recorded music during breaks?	
What are your fees for a 4-hour reception?	
What is your cost for each additional hour?	
Do you have liability insurance? What is your payment/cancellation policy?	

RECEPTION MUSIC COMPARISON CHART

POSSIBILITY 2	POSSIBILITY 3

RECEPTION MUSIC SELECTIONS

WHEN	Selection	Artist/Album	Played By
Receiving Line			
During Hors D'oeuvres			
During Dinner			
First Dance			
Second Dance			
Third Dance			
Bouquet Toss			
Garter Removal			
Garter Toss			
Cutting of the Cake			
Couple Leaving			
Other:			
Other:			
Other:			
Other:			
Other:			
Other:			
Other:			
Other:			

BAKERY

WEDDING CAKES MAY BE ORDERED FROM A CATERER OR FROM A BAKERY. Some hotels and restaurants may also be able to provide a wedding cake. However, you will probably be better off ordering your cake from a bakery that specializes in wedding cakes. Ask to see photographs of other wedding cakes your baker has created, and by all means, ask for a tasting!

WEDDING CAKE

Options: When ordering your cake, you will have to decide not only on a flavor, but also on a size, shape, and color. Size is determined by the number of guests. You can choose from one large tier to two, three, or more smaller tiers. The cake can be round, square, or heart-shaped. The most common flavors are chocolate, carrot, lemon, rum, and "white" cakes. You can be creative by adding a filling to your cake, such as custard, strawberry, or chocolate. You may also want to consider having tiers of different flavors.

Things to Consider: Price, workmanship, quality, and taste vary considerably from baker to baker. In addition to flavor, size, and cost, consider decoration and spoilage (sugar keeps longer than cream frostings). The cake should be beautifully displayed on its own table decorated with flowers or greenery. Make sure the baker, caterer, or reception site manager can provide you with a pretty cake-cutting knife. If not, you will need to purchase or rent one.

When determining the size of the cake, don't forget that you'll be saving the top tier for your first anniversary. This top tier should be removed before the cake is cut, wrapped in several layers of plastic wrap, or put inside a plastic container and kept frozen until your anniversary.

Tips to Save Money: Some bakers have set-up and delivery fees, some don't. Check for individuals who bake from their home. They are usually more reasonable, but you should check with your local health department before hiring one of these at-home bakers. Also, some caterers have contracts with bakeries and can pass on savings to you. Some bakeries require a deposit on columns and plates; other bakeries use disposable columns and plates, saving you the rental fee and the hassle of returning these items.

Price Range: $2.00 - $12/piece

BAKERY

GROOM'S CAKE

The groom's cake is an old southern tradition whereby this cake is cut up and distributed to guests in little white boxes engraved with the bride and groom's names. Today the groom's cake, if offered, is cut and served along with the wedding cake.

Options: Usually a chocolate cake decorated with fruit.

Tips to Save Money: Because of its cost and the labor involved in cutting and distributing the cake, very few people offer this delightful custom any more.

Price Range: $1.00 - $2.00/piece

CAKE DELIVERY/SET-UP FEE

This is the fee charged by bakers to deliver and set up your wedding cake at the reception site. It usually includes a deposit on the cake pillars and plate which will be refunded upon their return to the baker.

Tips to Save Money: Have a friend or family member get a quick lesson on how to set up your cake. Have them pick it up and set it up the day of your wedding, then have the florist decorate the cake and/or cake table with flowers and greenery.

Price Range: $40 - $100

CAKE-CUTTING FEE

Most reception sites and caterers charge a fee for each slice of cake they cut if the cake is brought in from an outside bakery. This fee will probably shock you. It is simply their way of enticing you to order the cake through them. And unfortunately, many caterers will not allow a member of your party to cut the cake.

Tips to Save Money: Many hotels and restaurants include a dessert in the cost of their meal packages. If you forego this dessert and substitute your cake as the dessert, they may be willing to waive the cake-cutting fee. Be sure to ask them.

Price Range: $0.75 - $2.50 per person

CAKE TOP

The bride's cake is often topped and surrounded with fresh flowers, but traditional "cake tops" (figurines set atop the wedding cake) are also very popular.

Options: Bells, love birds, a bridal couple or replica of two wedding rings are popular choices for cake tops and can be saved as mementos of your wedding day.

Beware: Some porcelain and other heavier cake tops need to be anchored down into the cake. If you're planning to use a cake top other than flowers, be sure to discuss this with your baker.

Tips to Save Money: Borrow a cake top from a friend or a family member as "something borrowed," an age-old wedding tradition (see page 223.)

Price Range: $20 - $150

CAKE KNIFE/TOASTING GLASSES

Your cake knife and toasting glasses should compliment your overall setting; these items will bring you happy memories of your wedding day every time you use them. The cake knife is used to cut the cake at the reception. The bride usually cuts the first two slices of the wedding cake with the groom's hand placed over hers. The groom feeds the bride first, then the bride feeds the groom. This tradition makes beautiful wedding photographs.

You will need toasting glasses to toast each other after cutting the cake. They are usually decorated with ribbons or flowers and kept near the cake. This tradition also makes beautiful wedding photographs.

Things to Consider: Consider having your initials and wedding date engraved on your wedding knife as a memento. Consider purchasing crystal or silver toasting glasses as a keepsake of your wedding. Have your florist decorate your knife and toasting glasses with flowers or ribbons.

Tips to Save Money: Borrow your cake knife or toasting glasses from a friend or family member as "something borrowed," an age-old wedding tradition (see page 223). Use the reception facility's glasses and knife, and decorate them with flowers or ribbon.

Price Range: $15 - $120/knife; $10 - $100/toasting glasses

BAKERY COMPARISON CHART

QUESTIONS	POSSIBILITY 1
What is the name of the bakery?	
What is the bakery's website and e-mail?	
What is the address of the bakery?	
What is the name and phone number of my contact person?	
How many years have you been making wedding cakes?	
What are your wedding cake specialties?	
Do you offer free tastings of your wedding cakes?	
Are your wedding cakes fresh or frozen?	
How far in advance should I order my cake?	
Can you make a groom's cake?	
Do you lend, rent, or sell cake knives?	
What is the cost per serving of my desired cake?	
What is your cake pillar and plate rental fee, if any?	
Is this fee refundable upon the return of these items?	
When must these items be returned?	
What is your cake delivery and set-up fee?	
What is your payment/cancellation policy?	

POSSIBILITY 2	POSSIBILITY 3

NOTES

FLOWERS

FLOWERS ADD BEAUTY, FRAGRANCE, AND COLOR TO YOUR WEDDING.
Like everything else, flowers should fit your overall style and color scheme. You can incorporate flowers in many different parts of your wedding from decorating the ceremony site, to using them as accents at place settings during the reception. You can also choose flowers that have special meaning or significance. Be sure to take into consideration the cost and availability when making your selection.

BRIDE'S BOUQUET

The bridal bouquet is one of the most important elements of the bride's attire and deserves special attention. Start by selecting the color and shape of the bouquet. The bridal bouquet should be carried low enough so that all the intricate details of your gown are visible.

Options: There are many colors, scents, sizes, shapes, and styles of bouquets to choose from. Popular styles are the cascade, cluster, contemporary, and hand-tied garden bouquets. The traditional bridal bouquet is made of white flowers. Stephanotis, gardenias, white roses, orchids, and lilies of the valley are popular choices for an all-white bouquet.

If you prefer a colorful bouquet, you may want to consider using roses, tulips, stock, peonies, freesia, and gerbera, which come in a wide variety of colors. Using scented flowers in your bouquet will evoke memories of your wedding day whenever you smell them in the future. Popular fragrant flowers are gardenias, freesia, stephanotis, bouvardia, and narcissus. Select flowers that are in season to ensure availability (see pages 177-178.)

Things to Consider: Your flowers should complement the season, your gown, your color scheme, your attendants' attire, and the style and formality of your wedding. If you have a favorite flower, build your bouquet around it and include it in all your arrangements. Some flowers carry centuries of symbolism. Consider stephanotis -- tradition regards it as the bridal good-luck flower! Pimpernel signifies change; white flowers radiate innocence; forget-me-nots indicate true love; and ivy stands for friendship, fidelity, and matrimony -- the three essentials for a happy marriage.

No flower, however, has as much symbolism for brides as the orange blossom, having at least 700 years of nuptial history. Its unusual ability to simultaneously bear flowers and produce fruit symbolizes the fusion of beauty, personality, and fertility.

Whatever flowers you select, final

arrangements should be made well in advance of your wedding date to ensure availability. Confirm your final order and delivery time a few days before the wedding. Have the flowers delivered before the photographer arrives so that you can include them in your pre-ceremony photos.

In determining the size of your bouquet, consider your gown and your overall stature. Carry a smaller bouquet if you're petite or if your gown is fairly ornate. A long, cascading bouquet complements a fairly simple gown or a tall or larger bride. Arm bouquets look best when resting naturally in the crook of your arm.

For a natural, fresh-picked look, have your florist put together a cluster of flowers tied together with a ribbon. For a Victorian appeal, carry a nosegay or a basket filled with flowers. Or carry a Bible or other family heirloom decorated with just a few flowers. For a contemporary look, you may want to consider carrying an arrangement of calla lilies or other long-stemmed flower over your arm. For a dramatic statement, carry a single stem of your favorite flower!

Beware: If your bouquet includes delicate flowers that will not withstand hours of heat or a lack of water, make sure your florist uses a bouquet holder to keep them fresh. If you want to carry fresh-cut stems without a bouquet holder, make sure the flowers you select are hardy enough to go without water for the duration of your ceremony and reception.

Tips to Save Money: The cost of some flowers may be significantly higher during their off-season. Try to select flowers which are in bloom and plentiful at the time of your wedding. Avoid exotic, out-of-season flowers. Allow your florist to emphasize your colors using more reasonable, seasonal flowers to achieve your overall look. If you have a favorite flower that is costly or out of season, consider using silk for that one flower.

Avoid scheduling your wedding on holidays such as Valentine's Day and Mother's Day when the price of flowers is higher. Because every attendant will carry or wear flowers, consider keeping the size of your wedding party down to accommodate your floral budget.

Price Range: $75 - $500

TOSSING BOUQUET

If you want to preserve your bridal bouquet, consider having your florist make a smaller, less expensive bouquet specifically for tossing. This will be the bouquet you toss to your single, female friends toward the end of the reception. Tradition has it that the woman who catches the bouquet is the next to be married. Have your florist include a few sprigs of fresh ivy in the tossing bouquet to symbolize friendship and fidelity.

Tips to Save Money: Use the floral cake top or guest book table "tickler bouquet" as the tossing bouquet. Or omit the tossing bouquet altogether and simply toss your bridal bouquet.

Price Range: $20 - $100

MAID OF HONOR'S BOUQUET

The maid of honor's bouquet can be somewhat larger or of a different color than the rest of the bridesmaids' bouquets. This will help to set her apart from the others.

Price Range: $25 - $100

BRIDESMAIDS' BOUQUETS

The bridesmaids' bouquets should complement the bridal bouquet, but are generally smaller in size. The size and color should coordinate with the bridesmaids' dresses and the overall style of the wedding. Bridesmaids' bouquets are usually identical.

Options: To personalize your bridesmaids' bouquets, insert a different flower in each of their bouquets to make a statement. For example, if one of your bridesmaids has been sad, give her a lily of the valley to symbolize the return of happiness. To tell a friend that you admire her, insert yellow jasmine. A pansy will let your friend know that you are thinking of her.

Things to Consider: Choose a bouquet style (cascade, cluster, contemporary, hand-tied) that compliments the formality of your wedding and the height of your attendants. If your bridesmaids will be wearing floral print dresses, select flowers that complement the floral print.

Tips to Save Money: Have your attendants carry a single stemmed rose, lily, or other suitable flower for an elegant look that also saves money.

Price Range: $25 - $100/bouquet

FLOWERS

MAID OF HONOR/BRIDESMAIDS' HAIRPIECE

For a garden-look, have your maid of honor and bridesmaids wear garlands of flowers in their hair. If so, your maid of honor can have a slightly different color or variety of flower to set her apart from the others.

Options: You may consider using artificial flowers for the hairpieces as long as they are in keeping with the flowers carried by members of the bridal party. Since it is not always easy to find good artificial blooms, other types of hairpieces may be more satisfactory, durable, and attractive.

Things to Consider: Flowers used for the hairpiece must be a sturdy and long-lived variety.

Price Range: $8.00 - $100/hairpiece

FLOWER GIRL'S HAIRPIECE

Flower girls often wear a wreath of flowers as a hairpiece.

Options: This is another place where artificial flowers may be used, but they must be in keeping with the flowers carried by members of the bridal party. Since it is not always easy to find good artificial blooms, other types of hairpieces may be more satisfactory, durable, and attractive.

Things to Consider: If the flowers used for the hairpiece are not a sturdy and long-lived variety, a ribbon, bow, or hat might be a safer choice.

Price Range: $8.00 - $75

BRIDE'S GOING AWAY CORSAGE

You may want to consider wearing a corsage on your going-away outfit. This makes for pretty photos as you and your new husband leave the reception for your honeymoon. Have your florist create a corsage which echoes the beauty of your bouquet.

Beware: Put a protective shield under lilies when using them as a corsage, as their anthers will easily stain fabric. Be careful when using Alstroemeria as a corsage, as its sap can be harmful if it enters the human bloodstream.

Tips to Save Money: Ask your florist if s/he can design your bridal bouquet in such a way that the center flowers may be removed and worn as a corsage. Or omit this corsage altogether.

Price Range: $10 - $50

FAMILY MEMBERS' CORSAGES

The groom is responsible for providing flowers for his mother, the bride's mother, and the grandmothers. The officiant, if female, may also be given a corsage to reflect her important role in the ceremony. The corsages don't have to be identical, but they should be coordinated with the color of their dresses.

Options: The groom may order flowers that can be pinned to a pocketbook or worn around a wrist. He should ask which style the women prefer, and if a particular color is needed to coordinate with their dresses. Gardenias, camellias, white orchids, or cymbidium orchids are excellent choices for corsages, as they go well with any outfit.

Things to Consider: The groom may also want to consider ordering corsages for other close family members, such as sisters and aunts. This will add a little to your floral expenses, but will make these female family members feel more included in your wedding and will let guests know that they are related to the bride and groom. Many women do not like to wear corsages, so the groom should check with the people involved before ordering the flowers.

Beware: Put a protective shield under lilies when using them as corsages, as their anthers will easily stain fabric. Be careful when using Alstroemeria as corsages, as its sap can be harmful if it enters the human bloodstream.

Tips to Save Money: Ask your florist to recommend reasonable flowers for corsages. Dendrobium orchids are reasonable and make lovely corsages.

Price Range: $10 - $35/corsage

GROOM'S BOUTONNIERE

The groom wears his boutonniere on the left lapel, nearest to his heart.

Options: Boutonnieres are generally a single blossom such as a rosebud, stephanotis, freesia, or a miniature carnation. If a rosebud is used for the wedding party, have the groom wear two rosebuds, or add a sprig of baby's breath to differentiate him from the groomsmen.

FLOWERS

Things to Consider: Consider using a small cluster of flowers instead of a single bloom for the groom's boutonniere.

Beware: Be careful when using Alstroemeria as a boutonniere, as its sap can be harmful if it enters the human bloodstream.

Tips to Save Money: Use mini-carnations rather than roses.

Price Range: $4.00 - $25

USHERS AND OTHER FAMILY MEMBERS' BOUTONNIERES

The groom gives each man in his wedding party a boutonniere to wear on his left lapel. The officiant, if male, may also be given a boutonniere to reflect his important role in the ceremony. The ring bearer may or may not wear a boutonniere, depending on his outfit. A boutonniere is more appropriate on a tuxedo than on knickers and knee socks.

Options: Generally, a single blossom such as a rosebud, freesia, or miniature carnation is used as a boutonniere.

Things to Consider: The groom should also consider ordering boutonnieres for other close family members such as fathers, grandfathers, and brothers. This will add a little to your floral expenses, but will make these male family members feel more included in your wedding and will let guests know that they are related to the bride and groom.

Beware: Be careful when using Alstroemeria as boutonnieres, as its sap can be harmful if it enters the human bloodstream.

Tips to Save Money: Use mini-carnations rather than roses.

Price Range: $3.00 - $15/boutonniere

MAIN ALTAR

The purpose of flowers at the main altar is to direct the guests' visual attention toward the front of the church or synagogue and to the bridal couple. Therefore, they must be seen by guests seated in the back. The flowers for the ceremony site can be as elaborate or as simple as you wish. Your officiant's advice, or that of the altar guild or florist, can be most helpful in choosing flowers for the altar and chancel.

Options: If your ceremony is outside, decorate the arch, gazebo, or other structure serving as the altar with flowers or greenery. In a Jewish ceremony, vows are said under a Chuppah, which is placed at the altar and covered with greens and fresh flowers.

Things to Consider: In choosing floral accents, consider the decor of your ceremony site. Some churches and synagogues are ornate enough and don't need extra flowers. Too many arrangements would get lost in the architectural splendor. Select a few dramatic showpieces that will complement the existing decor. Be sure to ask if there are any restrictions on flowers at the church or synagogue. Remember, decorations should be determined by the size and style of the building, the formality of the wedding, the preferences of the bride, the cost, and the regulations of the particular site.

Tips to Save Money: Decorate the ceremony site with greenery only. Candlelight and greenery are elegant in and of themselves. Use greenery and flowers from your garden. Have your ceremony outside in a beautiful garden or by the water, surrounded by nature's own splendor.

Price Range: $50 - $3,000

ALTAR CANDELABRA

In a candlelight ceremony, the candelabra may be decorated with flowers or greens for a dramatic effect.

Options: Ivy may be twined around the candelabra, or flowers may be strung to them.

Price Range: $50 - $200

AISLE PEWS

Flowers, candles, or ribbons are often used to mark the aisle pews and add color.

Options: A cluster of flowers, a cascade of greens, or a cascade of flowers and ribbons are all popular choices. Candles with adorning greenery add an elegant touch.

Things to Consider: Use hardy flowers that can tolerate being handled as pew ornaments. Gardenias and camellias, for example, are too sensitive to last long.

FLOWERS

Beware: Avoid using Allium in your aisle pew decorations as they have an odor of onions.

Tips to Save Money: It is not necessary to decorate all of the aisle pews, or any at all. To save money, decorate only the reserved family pews. Or decorate every second or third pew.

Price Range: $5.00 - $75/pew

RECEPTION SITE

Flowers are a beautiful way to personalize your reception. Flowers for the reception, like everything else, should fit your overall style and color scheme. They can help transform a stark reception hall into a warm, inviting and colorful room.

Things to Consider: Consider renting indoor plants or small trees to give your reception a garden-like atmosphere. Decorate them with twinkle lights to achieve a magical effect.

Tips to Save Money: You can save money by taking flowers from the ceremony to the reception site for decorations. However, you must coordinate this move carefully to avoid having your guests arrive at an undecorated reception room. Use greenery rather than flowers to fill large areas. Trees and garlands of ivy can give a dramatic impact for little money. Use greenery and flowers from your garden. Have your reception outside in a beautiful garden or by the water, surrounded by nature's own beauty.

Price Range: $300 - $3,000

HEAD TABLE

The head table is where the wedding party will sit during the reception. This important table should be decorated with a larger or more dramatic centerpiece than the guest tables.

Things to Consider: Consider using a different color or style of arrangement to set the head table apart from the other tables.

Beware: Avoid using highly fragrant flowers, such as narcissus, on tables where food is being served or eaten, as their fragrance may conflict with other aromas.

Tips to Save Money: Decorate the head table with the bridal and attendants' bouquets.

Price Range: $100 - $600

GUEST TABLES

At reception tables where guests are seated, a small flower arrangement may be placed on each table.

Things to Consider: The arrangements should complement the table linens and the size of the table, and should be kept low enough so as not to hinder conversation among guests seated across from each other.

Beware: Avoid using highly fragrant flowers, like Narcissus, on tables where food is being served or eaten, as their fragrance may conflict with other aromas.

Tips to Save Money: To keep the cost down and for less formal receptions, use small potted flowering plants placed in white baskets, or consider using dried or silk arrangements that you can make yourself and give later as gifts. Or place a wreath of greenery entwined with colored ribbon in the center of each table. Use a different colored ribbon at each table and assign your guests to tables by ribbon color instead of number.

Price Range: $10 - $100/table

BUFFET TABLE

If buffet tables are used, have some type of floral arrangement on the tables to add color and beauty to your display of food.

Options: Whole fruits and bunches of berries offer a variety of design possibilities. Figs add a festive touch. Pineapples are a sign of hospitality. Vegetables offer an endless array of options to decorate with. Herbs are yet another option in decorating. A mixture of rosemary and mint combined with scented geraniums makes a very unique table decoration.

Things to Consider: Depending on the size of the table, place one or two arrangements at each side.

Beware: Avoid placing certain flowers, such as carnations, snapdragons, or the star of Bethlehem, next to buffet displays of fruits or vegetables, as they are extremely sensitive to the gasses emitted by these foods.

Price Range: $50 - $500

PUNCH TABLE

Put an assortment of greens or a small arrangement of flowers at the punch table. See "Buffet Table."

Price Range: $10 - $100

CAKE TABLE

The wedding cake is often the central location at the reception. Decorate the cake table with flowers.

Tips to Save Money: Have your bridesmaids place their bouquets on the cake table during the reception, or decorate the cake top only and surround the base with greenery and a few loose flowers.

Price Range: $30 - $300

CAKE

Flowers are a beautiful addition to a wedding cake and are commonly seen spilling out between the cake tiers.

Things to Consider: Use only nonpoisonous flowers, and have your florist – not the caterer – design the floral decorations for your cake. A florist will be able to blend the cake decorations into your overall floral theme.

Price Range: $20 - $100

CAKE KNIFE

Decorate your cake knife with a white satin ribbon and flowers.

Things to Consider: Consider engraving the cake knife with your names and wedding date.

Price Range: $5.00 - $35

TOASTING GLASSES

Tie small flowers with white ribbon onto the stems of your champagne glasses. These wedding accessories deserve a special floral touch since they will most likely be included in your special photographs.

Things to Consider: Consider engraving your toasting glasses with your names and wedding date.

Price Range: $10 - $35

FLORAL DELIVERY/SET-UP

Most florists charge a fee to deliver flowers to the ceremony and reception sites and to arrange them on site.

Things to Consider: Make sure your florist knows where your sites are and at what time to arrive for set-up.

Price Range: $25 - $200

FLORIST COMPARISON CHART

QUESTIONS	POSSIBILITY 1
What is the name of the florist?	
What is the website and e-mail of the florist?	
What is the address of the florist?	
What is the name and phone number of my contact person?	
What are your business hours?	
How many years of professional floral experience do you have?	
What percentage of your business is dedicated to weddings?	
Do you have access to out-of-season flowers?	
Will you visit my wedding sites to make floral recommendations?	
Can you preserve my bridal bouquet?	
Do you rent vases and candleholders? Can you provide silk flowers?	
What is the cost of the desired bridal bouquet?	
What is the cost of the desired boutonniere?	
What is the cost of the desired corsage?	
Do you have liability insurance?	
What are your delivery/set-up fees?	
What is your payment/cancellation policy?	

FLORIST COMPARISON CHART

POSSIBILITY 2	POSSIBILITY 3

BOUQUETS AND FLOWERS

BRIDE'S BOUQUET

Color Scheme: _____

Style: _____

Flowers: _____

_____

_____

_____

Greenery: _____

Other (Ribbons, Etc.): _____

MAID OF HONOR'S BOUQUET

Color Scheme: _____

Style: _____

Flowers: _____

_____

_____

_____

Greenery: _____

Other (Ribbons, Etc.): _____

BRIDESMAIDS' BOUQUETS

Color Scheme: _____

Style: _____

Flowers: _____

_____

_____

_____

Greenery: _____

Other (Ribbons, Etc.): _____

FLOWER GIRL'S BOUQUET

Color Scheme:

Style:

Flowers:

Greenery:

Other (Ribbons, Etc.):

OTHER

Groom's Boutonnieres:

Ushers and Other Boutonnieres:

Mother of the Bride Corsage:

Mother of the Groom Corsage:

Altar or Chuppah:

Steps to Altar or Chuppah:

BOUQUETS AND FLOWERS

Pews:

Entrance to the Ceremony:

Entrance to the Reception:

Receiving Line:

Head Table:

Parents' Table:

Guest Tables:

Cake Table:

Serving Table (Buffet, Dessert):

Gift Table:

FLOWER	Winter	Spring	Summer	Fall
Allium		X	X	
Alstroemeria	X	X	X	X
Amaryllis	X		X	
Anemone	X	X		X
Aster	X	X	X	X
Baby's Breath	X	X	X	X
Bachelor's Button	X	X	X	X
Billy Buttons		X	X	
Bird of Paradise	X	X	X	X
Bouvardia	X	X	X	X
Calla Lily	X	X	X	X
Carnation	X	X	X	X
Celosia		X	X	
Chrysanthemum	X	X	X	X
Daffodils		X		
Dahlia			X	X
Delphinium			X	X
Eucalyptus	X	X	X	X
Freesia	X	X	X	X
Gardenia	X	X	X	X
Gerbera	X	X	X	X
Gladiolus	X	X	X	X
Iris	X	X	X	X
Liatris		X	X	X
Lily	X	X	X	X

FLOWERS AND THEIR SEASONS

FLOWER	Winter	Spring	Summer	Fall
Lily of the Valley		X		
Lisianthus		X	X	X
Narcissus	X	X		X
Nerine	X	X	X	X
Orchid (Cattleya)	X	X	X	X
Orchid (Cymbidium)	X	X	X	X
Peony		X		
Pincushion			X	
Protea	X			X
Queen Anne's Lace			X	
Ranunculas		X		
Rose	X	X	X	X
Saponaria			X	
Snapdragon		X	X	X
Speedwell			X	
Star of Bethlehem	X			X
Statice	X	X	X	X
Stephanotis	X	X	X	X
Stock	X	X	X	X
Sunflower		X	X	
Sweet Pea		X		
Tuberose			X	X
Tulip	X	X		
Waxflower	X	X		

DECORATIONS

DECORATIONS CAN ENHANCE YOUR WEDDING by unifying all of the components of your ceremony and reception. Decorations can range anywhere from floral arrangements, twinkling lights, and centerpieces, to more personal touches including seating cards, menus, favors, and more. Most items, from stationery to place settings, are purchased, or arranged based on the look and feel the bride wants for her wedding. For example, if the theme is Asian inspired, paper lanterns and take-out boxes can create beautiful "Japanese style" ambience.

TABLE CENTERPIECES

Each of the tables at your reception, including the head table, should be decorated with a centerpiece.

Options: Candles, mirrors, and flowers are popular choices for table centerpieces. However, the options are endless. Just be creative! An arrangement of shells, for example, makes a very nice centerpiece for a seaside reception. Votive candles set on top of a mirror make a romantic centerpiece for an evening reception.

A wreath of greenery woven with colored ribbon makes a delightful centerpiece. Use a different color ribbon at each table and have your guests seated according to ribbon color!

Things to Consider: Select a table centerpiece which complements your colors and/or setting. The centerpiece for the head table should be larger or more elaborate than for the other tables. Make sure that your centerpiece is kept low enough so as not to hinder conversation among guests seated across from each other. Consider using a centerpiece that your guests can take home as a memento of your wedding.

Tips to Save Money: Make your own table centerpieces using materials that are not expensive.

Price Range: $10 - $100 each

BALLOONS

Balloons are often used to decorate a reception site. A popular idea is to release balloons at the church or reception. This adds a festive, exciting, and memorable touch to your wedding. Balloons can be used to create an arch backdrop for the wedding cake or inexpensive centerpieces for the tables.

Things to Consider: Color coordinate your balloons to match your color scheme. Choose colors from your bouquet or your bridesmaids' dresses.

DECORATIONS

Balloons should be delivered and set-up well in advance – at least before the photographer shows up.

If you are planning to release balloons at the church or reception, check with your city. Releasing balloons in some cities might be illegal. Also make sure there are no wires where balloons can get entangled. If they do, you could be held responsible for damages or cleanup expenses.

Tips to Save Money: Balloons are less expensive than fresh flowers and can be used as a substitute for flowers to decorate the reception site.

Price Range: $75 - $500

TRANSPORTATION

IT IS CUSTOMARY FOR THE BRIDE AND HER FATHER TO RIDE to the ceremony site together on the wedding day. You may also include some or all members of your wedding party. Normally a procession to the church begins with the bride's mother and several of the bride's attendants in the first vehicle. If desired, you can provide a second vehicle for the rest of the attendants. The bride and her father will go in the last vehicle. This vehicle will also be used to transport the bride and groom to the reception site after the ceremony.

TRANSPORTATION

Options: There are various options for transportation. The most popular choice is a limousine since it is big and open and can accommodate several people as well as your bridal gown. You can also choose to rent a car that symbolizes your personality as a couple.

There are luxury cars such as Mercedes Benz, sports cars such as a Ferraris, and vintage vehicles such as 1950's Thunderbirds or 1930's Cadillacs. If your ceremony and reception sites are fairly close together, and if weather permits, you might want to consider a more romantic form of transportation, such as a horse-drawn carriage.

Things to Consider: In some areas of the country, limousines are booked on a 3-hour minimum basis.

Beware: Make sure the company you choose is fully licensed and has liability insurance. Do not pay the full amount until after the event.

Tips to Save Money: Consider hiring only one large limousine. This limousine can transport you, your parents and your attendants to the ceremony, and then you and your new husband from the ceremony to the reception.

Price Range: $35 - $100/hour

TRANSPORTATION COMPARISON CHART

QUESTIONS	POSSIBILITY 1
What is the name of the transportation service?	
What is the website and e-mail of the transportation service?	
What is the address of the transportation service?	
What is the name and phone number of my contact person?	
How many years have you been in business?	
How many vehicles do you have available?	
Can you provide a back-up vehicle in case of an emergency?	
What types of vehicles are available?	
What are the various sizes of vehicles available?	
How old are the vehicles?	
How many drivers are available?	
How do your drivers dress for weddings?	
Do you have liability insurance?	
What is the minimum amount of time required to rent a vehicle?	
What is the cost per hour? Two hours? Three hours?	
How much gratuity is expected?	
What is your payment/cancellation policy?	

TRANSPORTATION COMPARISON CHART

POSSIBILITY 2	POSSIBILITY 3

WEDDING DAY TRANSPORTATION

TO CEREMONY SITE

BRIDAL PARTY MEMBER	Pick up Time	Pick up Location	Vehicle/Driver
Bride			
Groom			
Bride's Parents			
Groom's Parents			
Bridesmaids			
Ushers			
Other Guests			
Other Guests			

TO RECEPTION SITE

BRIDAL PARTY MEMBER	Pick up Time	Pick up Location	Vehicle/Driver
Bride			
Groom			
Bride's Parents			
Groom's Parents			
Bridesmaids			
Ushers			
Other Guests			
Other Guests			

RENTAL ITEMS

NOT ALL ITEMS NEED TO BE PURCHASED for the ceremony and reception. There are many items that you have the option of renting, such as a tent, canopy, chairs, and linens for the reception. This allows you to host a reception in your own home, or in less traditional locations, such as an art museum, a local park, or at the beach. However, be sure to take into account the cost for all these rental items when creating your budget.

BRIDAL SLIP

The bridal slip is an undergarment which gives the bridal gown its proper shape.

Things to Consider: Be sure to wear the same slip you'll be wearing on your wedding day during your fittings. Many bridal salons rent slips. Schedule an appointment to pick up your slip one week before the wedding; otherwise, you run the risk of not having one available on your wedding day. If rented, the slip will have to be returned shortly after the wedding. Arrange for someone to do this for you within the allotted time.

Tips to Save Money: Rent a slip rather than purchasing one; chances are you will never use it again.

Price Range: $25 - $75

CEREMONY ACCESSORIES

Ceremony rental accessories are the additional items needed for the ceremony, but not included in the ceremony site fee.

Options: Ceremony rental accessories may include the following items:

Aisle Runner: A thin rug made of plastic, paper, or cloth extending the length of the aisle. It is rolled out after the mothers are seated, just prior to the processional. Plastic or paper doesn't work well on grass; but if you must use one of these types of runners, make sure the grass is clipped short.

Kneeling Cushion: A small cushion or pillow placed in front of the altar where the bride and groom kneel for their wedding blessing.

Arch (Christian): A white lattice or brass arch where the bride and groom exchange their vows, often decorated with flowers and greenery.

Chuppah (Jewish): Canopy under which a Jewish ceremony is performed, symbolizing cohabitation and consummation.

RENTAL ITEMS

You may also need to consider renting audio equipment, aisle stanchions, candelabras, candles, candle-lighters, chairs, heaters, a gift table, a guest book stand, and a canopy.

Things to Consider: If you plan to rent any accessories for your ceremony, make sure the rental supplier has been in business for a reasonable period of time and has a good reputation. Reserve the items you need well in advance. Find out the company's payment, reservation, and cancellation policies.

Some companies allow you to reserve emergency items such as heaters or canopies without having to pay for them unless needed, in which case you would need to call the rental company a day or two in advance to request the items. If someone else requests the items you have reserved, the company should give you the right of first refusal.

Tips to Save Money: When considering a ceremony outside of a church, figure the cost of rental items. Negotiate a package deal, if possible, by renting items for both the ceremony and the reception from the same supplier. Consider renting these items from your florist so you only have to pay one delivery fee.

Price Range: $100 - $500

TENT/CANOPY

A large tent or canopy may be required for receptions held outdoors to protect you and your guests from the sun or rain. Usually rented through party rental suppliers, tents and canopies can be expensive due to the labor involved in delivery and set-up.

Options: Tents and canopies come in different sizes and colors. Depending on the shape of your reception area, you may need to rent several smaller canopies rather than one large one. Contact several party rental suppliers to discuss the options.

Things to Consider: Consider this cost when making a decision between an outdoor and an indoor reception. In cooler weather, heaters may also be necessary.

Tips to Save Money: Shop early and compare prices with several party rental suppliers.

Price Range: $300 - $5,000

DANCE FLOOR

A dance floor will be provided by most hotels and clubs. However, if your reception site does not have a dance floor, you may need to rent one through your caterer or a party rental supplier.

Things to Consider: When comparing prices of dance floors, include the delivery and set-up fees.

Price Range: $100 - $600

TABLES/CHAIRS

You will have to provide tables and chairs for your guests if your reception site or caterer doesn't provide them as part of their package. For a full meal, you will have to provide tables and seating for all guests. For a cocktail reception, you only need to provide tables and chairs for approximately 30 to 50 percent of your guests. Ask your caterer or reception site manager for advice.

Options: There are various types of tables and chairs to choose from. The most commonly used chairs for wedding receptions are typically white wooden or plastic chairs. The most common tables for receptions are round tables that seat eight guests. The most common head table arrangement is several rectangular tables placed end-to-end to seat your entire wedding party on one side, facing your guests. Contact various party rental suppliers to find out what types of chairs and tables they carry, as well as their price ranges.

Things to Consider: When comparing prices of renting tables and chairs, include the cost of delivery and set-up.

Tips to Save Money: Attempt to negotiate free delivery and set-up with party rental suppliers in exchange for giving them your business.

Price Range: $3.00 - $10 per person

LINEN/TABLEWARE

You will also need to provide linens and tableware for your reception if your reception site or caterer does not provide them as part of their package.

Options: For a sit-down reception where the meal is served by waiters and waitresses, tables are usually set with a cloth (usually white, but may be color coordinated with the wedding), a centerpiece, and complete place settings. At a less formal buffet reception where guests serve themselves, tables are covered with a cloth, but place settings are not mandatory. The necessary plates and silverware may be located at the buffet table, next to the food.

Things to Consider: Linens and tableware depend on the formality of your reception. When comparing prices of linens and tableware, include the cost of delivery and set-up.

Price Range: $3.00 -$25 per person

HEATERS

You may need to rent heaters if your ceremony or reception will be held outdoors and if the temperature could drop below sixty-five degrees.

Options: There are electric and gas heaters, both of which come in different sizes. Gas heaters are more popular since they do not have unsightly and unsafe electric cords.

Price Range: $25 - $75

LANTERNS

Lanterns are often used at evening receptions.

Options: Many choices are available, from fire lanterns to electric ones.

Things to Consider: Consider the formality of the reception and choose the proper lighting to complement your decorations.

Price Range: $6.00 - $60/lamp

OTHER RENTAL ITEMS (TRASH CANS, GIFT TABLE, ETC.)

If your reception site or caterer doesn't provide them, you will need to purchase, rent, or borrow other miscellaneous items for your reception, such as trash cans, a gift table, trash bags, and so on.

Rental Items ❖ 189

RENTAL SUPPLIER COMPARISON CHART

QUESTIONS	POSSIBILITY 1
What is the name of the party rental supplier?	
What is the website and e-mail of the party rental supplier?	
What is the address of the party rental supplier?	
What is the name and phone number of my contact person?	
How many years have you been in business?	
What are your hours of operation?	
Do you have liability insurance?	
What is the cost per item needed?	
What is the cost of pick-up and delivery?	
What is the cost of setting up the items rented?	
When would the items be delivered?	
When would the items be picked up after the event?	
What is your payment policy?	
What is your cancellation policy?	
Other:	
Other:	
Other:	

RENTAL SUPPLIER COMPARISON CHART

POSSIBILITY 2	POSSIBILITY 3

CEREMONY EQUIPMENT CHECKLIST

RENTAL SUPPLIER: _____ Contact Person: _____

Website: _____

E-mail: _____

Address: _____

City: _____ State: _____ Zip Code: _____

Phone Number: _____ Hours: _____

Payment Policy: _____ Cancellation Policy: _____

Delivery Time: _____ Tear Down Time: _____

Set-up Time: _____ Pick-up Time: _____

Qty.	Item	Description	Price	Total
	Arch/Altar			
	Canopy (Chuppah)			
	Backdrops			
	Floor Candelabra			
	Candles			
	Candle lighters			
	Kneeling Bench			
	Aisle Stanchions			
	Aisle Runners			
	Guest Book Stand			
	Gift Table			
	Chairs			
	Audio Equipment			
	Lighting			
	Heating/Cooling			
	Umbrellas/Tents			
	Bug Eliminator			
	Coat/Hat Rack			
	Garbage Cans			

RECEPTION EQUIPMENT CHECKLIST

RENTAL SUPPLIER: _____ Contact Person: _____

Website: _____

E-mail: _____

Address: _____

City: _____ State: _____ Zip Code: _____

Phone Number: _____ Hours: _____

Payment Policy: _____ Cancellation Policy: _____

Delivery Time: _____ Tear Down Time: _____

Set-up Time: _____ Pick-up Time: _____

Qty.	Item	Description	Price	Total
	Audio Equipment			
	Cake Table			
	Candelabras/Candles			
	Canopies			
	Coat/Hat Rack			
	Dance Floor			
	Bug Eliminator			
	Garbage Cans			
	Gift Table			
	Guest Tables			
	Heating/Cooling			
	High/Booster Chairs			
	Lighting			
	Mirror Disco Ball			
	Place Card Table			
	Tents			
	Umbrellas			
	Visual Equipment			
	Wheelchair Ramp			

NOTES

GIFTS

GIFTS ARE A WONDERFUL WAY TO SHOW YOUR APPRECIATION to family, friends, members of your wedding party, and to all those who have assisted you in your wedding planning process. Usually brides and grooms like to exchange something small, yet meaningful. Keepsake items make wonderful gifts for members of the wedding party.

BRIDE'S GIFT

The bride's gift is traditionally given by the groom to the bride. It is typically a personal gift such as a piece of jewelry.

Options: A string of pearls, a watch, pearl earrings, or a gold chain with a heart-shaped charm holding photos of the two of you.

Things to Consider: This gift is not necessary and should be given only if budget allows.

Tips to Save Money: Consider omitting this gift. A pretty card from the groom proclaiming his eternal love for the bride is a very special yet inexpensive gift.

Price Range: $50 - $500

GROOM'S GIFT

The groom's gift is traditionally given by the bride to the groom.

Options: A nice watch, an elegant pen

set, or a dramatic photo of the bride framed in silver or crystal.

Things to Consider: This gift is not necessary and should be given only if budget allows.

Tips to Save Money: Consider omitting this gift. A pretty card from the bride proclaiming her eternal love for the groom is a very special yet inexpensive gift.

Price Range: $50 - $500

BRIDESMAIDS' GIFTS

Bridesmaids' gifts are given by the bride to her bridesmaids and maid of honor as a permanent keepsake of the wedding. The best gifts are those that can be used both during and after the wedding, such as jewelry.

Options: For bridesmaids' gifts, consider items of jewelry that can be worn during the wedding to give your wedding party a coordinated and elegant look. Choose the collection that most fits your style, then select the type and color of stone to match the color of your flowers and/or bridesmaids dresses. We believe this is the perfect bridesmaids' gift!

Things to Consider: Bridesmaids' gifts are usually presented at the bridesmaids' luncheon, if there is one, or at the rehearsal dinner. The gift to the maid of honor may be similar to the bridesmaids' gifts, but should be a bit more expensive.

Tips to Save Money: Ask your photographer to take, at no extra charge, professional portraits of each bridesmaid and her escort for use as bridesmaids' gifts. Select a beautiful background that will remind your bridesmaids of the occasion, such as your cake table. Put the photo in a pretty frame. This makes a very special, yet inexpensive gift for your attendants.

Price Range: $25 - $200/gift

USHERS' GIFTS

Ushers' gifts are given by the groom to his ushers as a permanent keepsake of the wedding.

Options: For ushers' gifts, consider fancy pen sets, wallets, leather belts, silver frames, watches, and desk clocks.

Things to Consider: The groom should deliver his gifts to the ushers at the bachelor party or at the rehearsal dinner. The gift to the best man may be similar to the ushers' gifts, but should be a bit more expensive.

Tips to Save Money: Negotiate with your photographer to take, at no extra charge, professional portraits of each usher and his escort for use as ushers' gifts. Select a beautiful background that will remind your ushers of the occasion, such as your cake table.

Price Range: $25 - $200/gift

PARTIES

WEDDINGS ARE OFTEN MUCH MORE THAN A DAY LONG CELEBRATION. There can be plenty of festivities before and even after the actual wedding day. Typically, the events that take place before a wedding include the engagement party, bridal shower, bachelor party, bridesmaids luncheon, and rehearsal dinner. Some couples also like to have a brunch the day after the wedding to relax and relive the previous evening's celebration.

ENGAGEMENT PARTY

The engagement party is generally thrown by the bride's family to celebrate the big news. Gifts are not required at this party.

Things to Consider: If your schedule won't allow for it, an engagement party is by no means a requirement.

Options: An engagement party is typically held in your parents' home; however, renting a space or having dinner in a nice restaurant are also acceptable.

BRIDAL SHOWER

Traditionally, your wedding shower is thrown by your maid of honor and bridesmaids, unless they are a member of your immediate family. Because a shower is a gift-giving occasion, it is not considered socially acceptable for anyone in your immediate family to host this event. If your mother or sisters wish to be involved, have them offer to help with the cost of the event or offer their home for it. The agenda usually includes some games and gift-opening. Be sure to have someone keep track of which gift is from whom.

Things to Consider: You may have several showers thrown for you. When creating your guest lists, be sure not to invite the same people to multiple showers (the exception being members of the wedding party, who may be invited to all showers without the obligation of bringing a gift.) Only include people who have been invited to the wedding – the only exception to this is a work shower, to which all coworkers may be invited, whether or not they are attending the wedding.

Options: Tea parties, spa days, cocktail parties, and traditional at-home events are all options – these days even men are being invited as coed showers become more and more popular! Generally an event is themed (lingerie, cooking, home decor) and the invitation should give guests an idea of what type of gift to bring.

PARTIES

BACHELOR PARTY

The bachelor party is a male-only affair typically organized by the best man. He is responsible for selecting the date and reserving the place and entertainment as well as inviting his male friends and family. Your best man should also assign responsibilities to the ushers, as they should help with the organization of this party.

Things to Consider: You often hear wild stories about bachelor parties being nights full of women and alcohol, however these stories are actually quite rare. Most of the time, they are all lies or a big exaggeration of what really happened. It is not uncommon for the guys invited to the bachelor party to create these wild stories and make a vow of never telling the truth about how boring the party really was! However, make this party a memorable one. Make sure you do something different and enjoy it!

Options: In the past, a typical bachelor party would start with the young bachelor and his friends getting together for dinner and drinking a fair amount of beer. After eating and drinking to their heart's content, they would then go bar-hopping or get together at someone's house to play games or watch sports. Going to exotic dancing locations was also popular for young bachelors. As the bachelor age group becomes older (the average bachelor today is 27), this tradition has changed a bit. Now a bachelor party can be as simple as a group of guys getting together for dinner and drinks.

Beware: Your best man should not plan your bachelor party for the night before the wedding, since chances are that you will consume a fair amount of alcohol and stay up late. You don't want to have a hangover or be exhausted during your wedding. It is much more appropriate to have the bachelor party two or three nights before the wedding. Tell your best man that you will be busy the night before the wedding, just in case he is planning to surprise you. Your best man should designate a driver for you and for those who will be drinking alcohol. Remember, you and your best man are responsible for the well-being of everybody invited to the party.

BRIDESMAIDS' LUNCHEON

The bridesmaids' luncheon is given by the bride for her bridesmaids. It is not a shower; rather, it is simply a time for good friends to get together formally before the bride changes her status from single to married.

Things to Consider: You can give your bridesmaids their gifts at this gathering.

Otherwise, plan to give them their gifts at the rehearsal dinner.

Price Range: $12 - $60 per person

REHEARSAL DINNER

It is customary that the groom's parents host a dinner party following the rehearsal, the evening before the wedding. The dinner usually includes the bridal party, their spouses or guests, both sets of parents, close family members, the officiant, and the wedding consultant and/or coordinator.

Options: The rehearsal dinner party can be held just about anywhere, from a restaurant, hotel, or private hall to the groom's parents' home.

Tips to Save Money: Restaurants specializing in Mexican food or pizza are fun yet inexpensive options.

Price Range: $10 - $100 per person

NOTES

MISCELLANEOUS

WITH ALL THAT IS INVOLVED IN PLANNING A WEDDING, it is easy to forget some simple, but necessary tasks. Be sure that you don't forget to consider or complete some of the following items.

NEWSPAPER ANNOUNCEMENTS

There are two types of announcements you can send to your local newspaper: one to announce your engagement, and one to announce your wedding.

For your engagement announcement, send information to the newspapers, along with a photograph, right after your engagement or at least four to six weeks before the wedding. The photograph is usually the head and shoulders of the engaged couple. The photograph should be wallet-sized or larger, black and white, and glossy. Call your local newspapers to ask about their requirements. Most papers will not take orders over the phone, so you will need to mail the information or deliver it personally.

For your wedding announcement, send information to the newspapers, along with a photograph of either the bride alone or the bridal couple, at least three weeks before the wedding. The photograph should be wallet-sized or larger, black and white, and glossy. Your photograph should show the way you will look the day of your wedding. The announcement should appear the day following the ceremony.

Things to Consider: If you and your fiancé grew up in different towns, consider sending announcements to the local papers of both towns. If either of you is having second thoughts about the wedding, cancel both announcements as soon as possible.

Tips to Save Money: If you don't mind having your wedding announced a few weeks after the wedding, you can send a photo from your actual wedding day. This will save you the cost and hassle of dressing up to have your photo taken before the wedding.

Price Range: $40 - $100 (depending on size)

MARRIAGE LICENSE

Marriage license requirements are state-regulated and may be obtained from the County Clerk in most county courthouses.

Options: Some states (California and Nevada, for example) offer two types of marriage licenses: a public license and a confidential one. The public license is the most common one and requires a health certificate and a blood test. It can only be obtained at the County Clerk's office.

The confidential license is usually less expensive and does not require a health certificate or blood test. If offered, it can usually be obtained from most Justices of the Peace. An oath must be taken in order to receive either license.

Things to Consider: Requirements vary from state to state but generally include the following points:

>1. Applying for and paying the fee for the marriage license. There is usually a waiting period before the license is valid and a limited time before it expires.

>2. Meeting residency requirements for the state and/or county where the ceremony will take place.

>3. Meeting the legal age requirements for both bride and groom or having parental consent.

>4. Presenting any required identification, birth or baptismal certificates, marriage eligibility, or other documents.

>5. Obtaining a medical examination and/or blood test for both the bride and groom to detect communicable diseases.

Price Range: $20 - $100

PRENUPTIAL AGREEMENT

A prenuptial agreement is a legal contract between the bride and groom itemizing the property each brings into the marriage and explaining how those properties will be divided in case of divorce or death. Although you can write your own agreement, it is advisable to have an attorney draw up or review the document. The two of you should be represented by different attorneys.

Things to Consider: Consider a prenuptial agreement if one or both of you have a significant amount of capital or assets, or if there are children involved from a previous marriage. If you are going to live in a different state after the wedding, consider having an attorney from that state draw up or review your document.

Nobody likes to talk about divorce or death when planning a wedding, but it is very important to give these issues your utmost consideration. By drawing a prenuptial agreement, you encourage open communication and get a better idea of each other's needs and expectations. You should also consider drawing up or reviewing your wills at this time.

Tips to Save Money: Some software packages allow you to write your own will and prenuptial agreement, which can save you substantial attorney's fees. However, if you decide to draw either agreement on your own, you should still have an attorney review it.

Price Range: $500 - $3,000

BRIDAL GOWN PRESERVATION

The pride and joy you will experience in seeing your daughter and/or granddaughter wear your wedding gown on her wedding day will more than justify the expense of having your gown preserved. Bring your gown to a reputable dry cleaning company which specializes in preserving wedding gowns. They will dry clean your dress, vacuum seal it, and place it in an attractive box. By doing this, your gown will be protected from yellowing, falling apart, or getting damaged over the years. Most boxes have a plastic see-through window where you can show the top part of your dress to friends and family members without having to open the vacuum-sealed container.

Tips to Save Money: Some bridal boutiques offer gown preservation. Try to negotiate having your gown preserved for free with the purchase of a wedding gown. It's well worth the try! But remember, get any agreement in writing and be sure to have it signed by either the owner or the manager of the boutique.

Price Range: $100 - $250

BRIDAL BOUQUET PRESERVATION

The bridal bouquet can be preserved to make a beautiful memento of the wedding.

Things to Consider: Have your bouquet dried, mounted, and framed to hang on your wall or to display on an easel in a quiet corner of your home. You can also have an artist paint your bouquet.

Price Range: $100 - $500

MISCELLANEOUS

WEDDING CONSULTANT

Wedding consultants are professionals whose training, expertise, and contacts will help make your wedding as close to perfect as it can possibly be. They can save you considerable time, money and stress when planning your wedding. Wedding consultants have information on many ceremony and reception sites, as well as reliable service providers such as photographers, videographers, and florists, which will save you hours of investigation and legwork.

Wedding consultants can provide facilities and service providers to match your budget. They can also save you stress by ensuring that what you are planning is correct and that the service providers you hire are reliable and professional. Most service providers recommended by wedding consultants will go out of their way to do an excellent job for you so that the wedding consultant will continue to recommend their services.

Options: You can have a wedding consultant help you do as much or as little as you think necessary. A consultant can help you plan the whole event from the beginning to the end, helping you formulate a budget and select your ceremony, and reception sites, flowers, wedding gown, invitations, and service providers; and/or s/he can help you at the end by coordinating the rehearsal and the wedding day. Remember, you want to feel like a guest at your own wedding. You and your family should not have to worry about any details on your special day. This is the wedding consultant's job!

Things to Consider: Strongly consider engaging the services of a wedding consultant. Contrary to what many people believe, a wedding consultant is part of your wedding budget, not an extra expense! A good wedding consultant should be able to save you at least the amount of his/her fee by suggesting less expensive alternatives that still enhance your wedding. In addition, many consultants obtain discounts from the service providers they work with. If this is not enough, they are more than worth their fee by serving as an intermediary between you and your parents and/or service providers.

When hiring a wedding consultant, make sure you check his/her references. Ask the consultant if s/he is a member of the Association of Bridal Consultants (ABC) and ask to see a current membership certificate. All ABC members agree to uphold a Code of Ethics and Standards of Membership. Many consultants have formal training and experience in event planning and in other specialties related to weddings, such as flower arranging and catering.

Price Range: $500 - $10,000

WEDDING PLANNING ONLINE

With a computer and an internet connection, you can ease the process of planning your wedding. A good wedding planning website will help you create a budget, select your service providers, generate a guest list, address invitations, create a wedding timeline or schedule of events, keep track of payments made, keep track of invitations sent, as well as RSVPs and gifts received, and much more. You can even create your registry or a personal webpage or website all about your wedding!

Options: Wedding Solutions Publishing has a great wedding planning site that follows hand-in-hand with this book! Go to www.WeddingSolutions.com and plan your entire wedding with our online tools.

TAXES

Don't forget to figure-in the cost of taxes on all taxable items you purchase for your wedding. Many people make a big mistake by not figuring out the taxes they will have to pay for their wedding expenses. For example, if you are planning a reception for 250 guests with an estimated cost of $60/person for food and beverages, your pretax expenses would be $15,000. A sales tax of 7.5% would mean an additional expense of $1,125! Find out what the sales tax is in your area and which items are taxable, and figure this expense into your overall budget.

CONSULTANTS COMPARISON CHART

QUESTIONS	POSSIBILITY 1
What is the name of the wedding consultant?	
What is the website and e-mail of the wedding consultant?	
What is the address of the wedding consultant?	
What is the phone number of the wedding consultant?	
How many years of professional experience do you have?	
How many consultants are in your company?	
Are you a member of the Association of Bridal Consultants?	
What services do you provide?	
What are your hourly fees?	
What is your fee for complete wedding planning?	
What is your fee to oversee the rehearsal and wedding day?	
What is your payment policy?	
What is your cancellation policy?	
Do you have liability insurance?	
Other:	
Other:	
Other:	

CONSULTANTS COMPARISON CHART

POSSIBILITY 2	POSSIBILITY 3

CONSULTANT'S INFORMATION FORM

Make a copy of this form and give it to your wedding consultant.

THE WEDDING OF: _____

Ceremony Site: _____ Phone Number: _____

Ceremony Address: _____

Website: _____ E-mail: _____

Reception Site: _____ Phone Number: _____

Reception Address: _____

Website: _____ E-mail: _____

CEREMONY SERVICES	Contact Person	Arrive	Depart	Phone
Florist:				
Musicians:				
Officiant:				
Photographer:				
Rental Supplier:				
Site Coordinator:				
Soloist:				
Transportation:				
Videographer:				
Other:				

RECEPTION SERVICES	Contact Person	Arrive	Depart	Phone
Baker:				
Bartender:				
Caterer:				
Florist:				
Gift Attendant:				
Guest Book Attendant:				
Musicians:				
Rental Supplier:				
Site Coordinator:				
Transportation:				
Valet Service:				

NAME & ADDRESS CHANGE FORM

TO WHOM IT MAY CONCERN:

This is to inform you of my recent marriage and to request a change of name and/or address. The following information will be effective as of: _____

My account/policy number is: _____

Under the name of: _____

PREVIOUS INFORMATION:

Husband's Name: _____ Phone No: _____

Previous Address: _____

Wife's Maiden Name: _____ Phone No: _____

Previous Address: _____

NEW INFORMATION:

Husband's Name: _____ Phone No: _____

Wife's Name: _____ Phone No: _____

New Address: _____

SPECIAL INSTRUCTIONS:

❑ Change name

❑ Change address/phone

❑ Add spouse's name

❑ Send necessary forms to include my spouse on my policy/account

❑ We plan to continue service

❑ We plan to discontinue service after: _____

If you have any questions, please feel free to contact us at: ( ) _____

Husband's Signature: _____

Wife's Signature: _____

CHANGE OF ADDRESS WORKSHEET

COMPANY	Account/Policy No.	Phone or Address	Done
Auto Insurance	_____	_____	_____
Auto Registration	_____	_____	_____
Bank Accounts	_____	_____	_____
	_____	_____	_____
	_____	_____	_____
	_____	_____	_____
Credit Cards	_____	_____	_____
	_____	_____	_____
	_____	_____	_____
	_____	_____	_____
	_____	_____	_____
Dentist	_____	_____	_____
	_____	_____	_____
Doctors	_____	_____	_____
	_____	_____	_____
	_____	_____	_____
Driver's License	_____	_____	_____
	_____	_____	_____
Employee Records	_____	_____	_____
	_____	_____	_____
Insurance: Dental	_____	_____	_____
Insurance: Disability	_____	_____	_____
Insurance: Homeowner's	_____	_____	_____
Insurance: Life	_____	_____	_____
Insurance: Renters	_____	_____	_____
Insurance: Other	_____	_____	_____
IRA Accounts	_____	_____	_____
	_____	_____	_____
Leases	_____	_____	_____
	_____	_____	_____
Loan Companies	_____	_____	_____
	_____	_____	_____
	_____	_____	_____

CHANGE OF ADDRESS WORKSHEET

COMPANY	Account/Policy No.	Phone or Address	Done
Memberships	_____	_____	_____
	_____	_____	_____
	_____	_____	_____
Mortgage	_____	_____	_____
Newspaper	_____	_____	_____
	_____	_____	_____
	_____	_____	_____
Passport	_____	_____	_____
Pensions	_____	_____	_____
Post Office	_____	_____	_____
	_____	_____	_____
Property Title	_____	_____	_____
	_____	_____	_____
Retirement Accounts	_____	_____	_____
	_____	_____	_____
Safe Deposit Box	_____	_____	_____
School Records	_____	_____	_____
	_____	_____	_____
	_____	_____	_____
Social Security	_____	_____	_____
	_____	_____	_____
Stock Broker	_____	_____	_____
Subscriptions	_____	_____	_____
	_____	_____	_____
Taxes	_____	_____	_____
	_____	_____	_____
Phone Company	_____	_____	_____
Utilities	_____	_____	_____
Voter Registration	_____	_____	_____
	_____	_____	_____
Will/Trust	_____	_____	_____
Other	_____	_____	_____
	_____	_____	_____

NOTES

TIMELINES

THE FOLLOWING SECTION INCLUDES TWO DIFFERENT TIMELINES or schedules of events for your wedding day: one for members of your wedding party and one for the various service providers you have hired. Use these timelines to help your wedding party and service providers understand their roles and where they need to be throughout your wedding day. This will also give you a much better idea of how your special day will unfold.

When preparing your timeline, first list the time that your wedding ceremony will begin. Then work forward or backwards, using the sample as your guide. The samples included give you an idea of how much time each event typically takes. But feel free to change the amount of time allotted for any event when customizing your own.

WEDDING PARTY TIMELINE (SAMPLE)

This is a sample wedding party timeline. To develop your own, use the form on pages 216-217. Use the extra space in the description column to write additional information such as addresses or any other comments that will help members of your wedding party understand what their roles are. Once you have created your own timeline, make a copy and give one to each member of your wedding party.

TIME	DESCRIPTION	BRIDE	BRIDE'S MOTHER	BRIDE'S FATHER	MAID OF HONOR	BRIDE'S MAIDS	BRIDE'S FAMILY	GROOM	GROOM'S MOTHER	GROOM'S FATHER	BEST MAN	USHERS	GROOM'S FAMILY	FLOWER GIRL	RING BEARER
2:00 PM	Manicurist Appointment:	✓	✓		✓	✓									
2:30 PM	Hair/Makeup Appointment:	✓	✓		✓	✓									
4:15 PM	Arrive at Dressing Site:	✓	✓		✓	✓									
4:30 PM	Arrive at Dressing Site:							✓			✓	✓			
4:45 PM	Pre-Ceremony Photos:							✓	✓	✓	✓	✓	✓		
5:15 PM	Arrive at Ceremony Site:							✓	✓	✓	✓	✓	✓		
5:15 PM	Pre-Ceremony Photos:	✓	✓	✓	✓	✓	✓								
5:20 PM	Give Officiant Marriage License & Fee:										✓				
5:20 PM	Ushers receive seating chart											✓			
5:30 PM	Ushers hand out wedding program as guests arrive											✓			
5:30 PM	Arrive at ceremony site:													✓	✓
5:30 PM	Guest book attendant asks guests to sign in:														
5:30 PM	Prelude Music Begins:														
5:35 PM	Begin Seating Guests:											✓			
5:45 PM	Arrive at ceremony site:	✓	✓	✓	✓	✓	✓								
5:45 PM	Honored Guests are Seated:											✓			
5:50 PM	Groom's Parents are Seated								✓	✓		✓			
5:55 PM	Bride's Mother is Seated		✓									✓			
5:55 PM	Attendants line up and get ready for Procession				✓	✓						✓		✓	✓
5:56 PM	Bride's father takes his place next to Bride	✓		✓											
5:57 PM	Aisle Runner is rolled down the aisle											✓			
5:58 PM	Officiant, Groom, and Best Man enter from:							✓			✓				
6:00 PM	Processional music begins:														

TIME	DESCRIPTION	BRIDE	BRIDE'S MOTHER	BRIDE'S FATHER	MAID OF HONOR	BRIDE'S MAIDS	BRIDE'S FAMILY	GROOM	GROOM'S MOTHER	GROOM'S FATHER	BEST MAN	USHERS	GROOM'S FAMILY	FLOWER GIRL	RING BEARER
6:00 PM	Groom's Mother Stands up								✓						
6:01 PM	Ushers enter from:											✓			
6:02 PM	Bridesmaids, Maid of Honor, RB, FG, Bride & Father march up aisle	✓		✓	✓	✓								✓	✓
6:20 PM	Bride/Groom, FG/RB, Maid of Honor/Best Man march down aisle	✓			✓			✓			✓			✓	✓
6:22 PM	Mother/Father of Bride, Mother/Father of Groom march down aisle		✓	✓					✓	✓					
6:25 PM	Signing of Marriage Certificate:	✓			✓			✓			✓				
6:30 PM	Post ceremony photos taken:	✓	✓	✓	✓	✓	✓	✓	✓	✓	✓	✓	✓	✓	✓
6:30 PM	Cocktails and Hors D'oeuvres served:														
6:30 PM	Gift attendant watches over gifts as guests arrive:														
7:15 PM	Receiving Line is formed, or Band/DJ announces Bride & Groom	✓						✓							
7:45 PM	Guests are seated & meal is served														
8:30 PM	Toasts										✓				
8:40 PM	First Dance	✓						✓							
8:45 PM	Traditional Dances:	✓	✓	✓				✓	✓	✓					
9:00 PM	Open dance floor for all guests														
9:30 PM	Bride & groom toast eachother before cutting cake	✓						✓							
9:40 PM	Cake-cutting ceremony	✓						✓							
10:00 PM	Bride tosses bouquet to single women	✓			✓	✓								✓	
10:10 PM	Groom takes garter from Bride's leg	✓						✓							
10:15 PM	Groom tosses garter to single men							✓			✓	✓			✓
10:20 PM	Man who caught garter puts on woman's leg who caught bouquet														
10:30 PM	Hand out rose petals, rice, or birdseed to toss over bride & groom as they														
10:45 PM	Grand Exit by Bride & Groom	✓						✓							

WEDDING PARTY TIMELINE

Create your own timeline using this form.
Make copies,and give one to each member of your wedding party.

TIME	DESCRIPTION	BRIDE	BRIDE'S MOTHER	BRIDE'S FATHER	MAID OF HONOR	BRIDE'S MAIDS	BRIDE'S FAMILY	GROOM	GROOM'S MOTHER	GROOM'S FATHER	BEST MAN	USHERS	GROOM'S FAMILY	FLOWER GIRL	RING BEARER

WEDDING PARTY TIMELINE

Create your own timeline using this form.
Make copies and give one to each member of your wedding party.

TIME	DESCRIPTION	BRIDE	BRIDE'S MOTHER	BRIDE'S FATHER	MAID OF HONOR	BRIDE'S MAIDS	BRIDE'S FAMILY	GROOM	GROOM'S MOTHER	GROOM'S FATHER	BEST MAN	USHERS	GROOM'S FAMILY	FLOWER GIRL	RING BEARER

This is a sample of a service provider timeline. To develop your own, use the form on pages 220-221. Use the extra space in the description column to write additional information such as addresses or any other comments that will help your service providers understand what their roles are and where they should be throughout the day. Once you have created your own timeline, make a copy and give one to each of your service providers.

TIME	DESCRIPTION	BAKERY	CATERER	CEREM. MUSICIAN	OFFICIANT	OTHER	FLORIST	HAIR DRESSER	LIMOUSINE	MAKEUP ARTIST	MANICURIST	PARTY RENTALS	PHOTOGRAPHER	RECEP. MUSICIANS	VIDEOGRAPHER
1:00 PM	Party rental supplier drops off supplies at ceremony site:											✓			
1:30 PM	Party rental supplier drops off supplies at reception site:											✓			
2:00 PM	Manicurist meets bride at:										✓				
2:30 PM	Makeup artist meets bride at:									✓					
3:00 PM	Hair dresser meets bride at:							✓							
4:00 PM	Limousine picks up bridal party at:								✓						
4:15 PM	Caterer begins setting up:		✓												
4:30 PM	Florist arrives at ceremony site:						✓								
4:40 PM	Baker delivers cake to reception site:	✓													
4:45 PM	Florist arrives at reception site:						✓								
4:45 PM	Pre-ceremony photos of groom's family at:												✓		
5:00 PM	Videographer arrives at ceremony site:														✓
5:15 PM	Pre-ceremony photos of bride's family at:												✓		
5:20 PM	Ceremony site decorations are completed (guest book table, flowers, etc)					✓	✓								
5:30 PM	Prelude music begins:			✓											
5:45 PM	Reception site decorations completed (gift table, place cards, flowers, etc)	✓				✓	✓								
5:58 PM	Officiant enters from:				✓										
6:00 PM	Processional music begins:			✓											
6:15 PM	Caterer finishes setting up:		✓												
6:25 PM	Bride & Groom sign marriage certificate				✓								✓		✓
6:30 PM	Post-ceremony photos of wedding party at:												✓		
6:30 PM	Cocktails & Hors D'oeuvres served:		✓												
6:30 PM	Band/DJ starts playing:													✓	

TIME	DESCRIPTION	BAKERY	CATERER	CEREM. MUSICIAN	OFFICIANT	OTHER	FLORIST	HAIR DRESSER	LIMOUSINE	MAKEUP ARTIST	MANICURIST	PARTY RENTALS	PHOTOGRAPHER	RECEP. MUSICIANS	VIDEOGRAPHER
6:30 PM	Move guest book & gifts to reception site						✓								
6:30 PM	Ceremony music ends			✓											
6:45 AM	Move arch/urns/flowers to reception site						✓								
7:00 PM	Limousine picks up Bride & Groom at ceremony site:								✓						
7:15 PM	Band/DJ announces entrance of Bride & Groom													✓	
7:45 PM	Meal is served		✓												
8:10 PM	Band/DJ announces champagne will be served for toasts													✓	
8:15 PM	Champagne is served for toasts		✓												
8:30 PM	Band/DJ announces toast by Best Man													✓	
8:40 PM	Band/DJ announces first dance													✓	
9:00 PM	Transport gifts to:						✓								
9:30 PM	Band/DJ announces cake-cutting ceremony													✓	
10:30 PM	Transport top tier of cake & flowers to:						✓								
10:40 PM	Transport rental items that need to be returned to:						✓								
10:45 PM	Limousine picks up Bride & Groom at reception site:								✓						
11:00 PM	Videographer departs														✓
11:00 PM	Photographer departs												✓		
11:00 PM	Wedding consultant departs						✓								
11:30 PM	Band/DJ stops playing													✓	
11:45 PM	Party rental supplier picks up supplies at ceremony/reception sites											✓			

SERVICE PROVIDER TIMELINE

Create your own timeline using this form.
Make copies and give one to each of your service providers.

TIME	DESCRIPTION	BAKERY	CATERER	CEREM. MUSICIAN	OFFICIANT	OTHER	FLORIST	HAIR DRESSER	LIMOUSINE	MAKEUP ARTIST	MANICURIST	PARTY RENTALS	PHOTOGRAPHER	RECEP. MUSICIANS	VIDEOGRAPHER

SERVICE PROVIDER TIMELINE

Create your own timeline using this form.
Make copies and give one to each of your service providers.

TIME	DESCRIPTION	BAKERY	CATERER	CEREM. MUSICIAN	OFFICIANT	OTHER	FLORIST	HAIR DRESSER	LIMOUSINE	MAKEUP ARTIST	MANICURIST	PARTY RENTALS	PHOTOGRAPHER	RECEP. MUSICIANS	VIDEOGRAPHER

NOTES

WEDDING TRADITIONS

HAVE YOU EVER WONDERED WHY CERTAIN THINGS are almost always done at weddings? For example, why the bride carries a bouquet or wears a veil? Or why guests throw rice or rose petals over the newlyweds? In this section, we discuss the origin and symbolism of some of the most popular wedding traditions.

This comprehensive list of traditions comes from a delightful little book entitled *The Romance of the Wedding Ceremony* by Rev. Richleigh Hale Powers, Ph.D. This easy-to-use book has helped many couples personalize their wedding ceremony.

THE BRIDE'S BOUQUET

In history, a bride carried her bouquet for protective reasons – carrying strong-smelling spices or garlic could help to drive away evil spirits which might plague the wedding. Eventually the floral bouquet became prevalent and symbolized fertility and the hope for a large family. Each flower was assigned a particular meaning when carried in a bride's bouquet.

THE BRIDE'S VEIL

The veil has historically symbolized virginity and innocence. It is believed that in ancient times, a bride was veiled to protect her from evil spirits or to shield her from her husband's eyes –

arranged marriages were common and often they were not to officially meet until AFTER the wedding.

RICE AND PETALS

The tossing of rice began to aid with fertility, both for the couple and for their harvest.

SOMETHING OLD, SOMETHING NEW, SOMETHING BORROWED, SOMETHING BLUE

Something old is carried to represent the history of the bride and ties her to her family. Something new represents the future and the bride's ties to her new family. Something borrowed should come from someone who is happily married and is carried in the hopes that their good fortune may rub off on you. Blue is the color of purity and is carried to represent faithfulness in the marriage. Many people don't realize that there is one more item – a sixpence in your shoe – which represents wealth.

WEDDING TRADITIONS

WHITE AISLE RUNNER

Using a white aisle runner symbolizes bringing God into your union and is indicative of walking on holy ground.

SPECIAL SEATING FOR THE FAMILIES

The families are traditionally seated on opposite sides of the church, because in ancient times families would often have a wedding in order to bring peace to warring clans. In order to prevent fighting from taking place during the wedding, they were kept separated.

THE GROOM ENTERING FIRST

Traditionally, the groom enters first, and gives his vows first, because he is considered to be the one who has initiated the wedding.

THE FATHER OF THE BRIDE WALKING DOWN THE AISLE

In historic times, brides were literally given away by their fathers – women were betrothed, often at birth, to men they did not know and their parents were able to "give them away." Now, giving the bride away is simply a way for the bride's family to publicly show their support of the union.

THE BRIDE STANDING ON THE LEFT

Because times were so violent and unpredictable, in ancient times a bride was likely to be kidnapped and held for ransom at her wedding! The bride was placed on the groom's left in order to leave his sword-hand free in case he had to defend her.

THE SYMBOLISM OF THE WEDDING RINGS

The circle of the wedding ring represents eternal love and devotion. The Greeks believed that the fourth finger on the left hand has a vein which leads directly to the heart, so this is the finger onto which we place these bands.

KISSING THE BRIDE

During the Roman empire, the kiss between a couple symbolized a legal bond – hence the expression "sealed with a kiss." Continued use of the kiss to seal the marriage bond is based on the deeply rooted idea of the kiss as a vehicle for transference of power and souls.

THE COUPLE BEING PRONOUNCED "HUSBAND AND WIFE"

This establishes their change of names and a definite point in time for the beginning of the marriage. These words are to remove any doubt in the minds of the couple or the witnesses concerning the validity of the marriage.

SIGNING THE WEDDING PAPERS

The newlywed couple signs the wedding papers to establish a public document and a continuing public record of the covenant.

SIGNING THE GUEST BOOK

Your wedding guests are official witnesses to the covenant. By signing the guest book they are saying, "I have witnessed the vows, and I will testify to the reality of this marriage." Because of this significance, the guest book should be signed after the wedding rather than before it.

THE PURPOSE OF THE RECEIVING LINE

The receiving line is for guests to give their blessings to the couple and their parents.

THE BRIDE AND GROOM FEEDING WEDDING CAKE TO EACH OTHER

This represents the sharing of their body to become one. A New Testament illustration of this symbolism is The Lord's Supper.

NOTES

_____

_____

_____

_____

_____

_____

_____

_____

_____

_____

_____

_____

_____

_____

_____

_____

_____

_____

_____

_____

_____

_____

_____

_____

_____

_____

_____

_____

_____

_____

_____

DO'S & DON'TS

YOUR WEDDING WILL LAST ONLY A FEW HOURS, but will likely take several months to plan. That is why it is so important to enjoy the complete wedding planning process. This is a time to get excited, to fall even more deeply in love with each other, to learn more about each other, and a time to compromise. If you can handle planning your wedding with your fiancé and parents, you can handle anything! Here is a list of do's and don'ts when planning your special day. If you follow these suggestions, your wedding planning and your wedding day will be much more enjoyable!

DO'S

- Read this book completely.

- Hire a professional wedding consultant.

- Maintain a sense of humor.

- Maintain open communication with your fiancé and with both sets of parents, especially if they are financing the wedding.

- Be receptive to your parents' ideas, especially if they are financing the wedding.

- Be flexible and keep your overall budget in mind.

- Maintain a regular routine of exercise and eat a well-balanced diet.

- Buy the *Ultimate Groom's Guide*, published by Wedding Solutions Publishing, Inc., and give it to your fiancé. Available for purchase at all major bookstores.

- Buy the *Wedding Party Responsibility Cards*, published by Wedding Solutions Publishing, and give a card to each member of your wedding party. Available for purchase at all major book stores.

- Register for gifts; consider a price range that your guests can afford.

- Break-in your shoes well before your wedding day.

DO'S & DON'TS

DO'S (CONT'S)

- Practice with makeup and various hairstyles for your wedding day.

- Check recent references for all of your service providers.

- Get everything in writing with your service providers.

- Assign your guests to tables and group them together by age, interests, acquaintances, etc.

- Consider drawing-up a prenuptial agreement and a will.

- Send thank-you notes as soon as you receive gifts.

- Give a rose to each of your mothers as you walk down the aisle during the recessional.

- Try to spend some time with each of your guests and personally thank them for coming to your wedding.

- Encourage the bride's parents to introduce their family and friends to the family and friends of the groom's family, and vice-versa.

- Toast both sets of parents at the rehearsal dinner and/or at the reception. Thank them for everything they have done for you and for giving you a beautiful wedding.

- Eat well at the reception, especially if you will be drinking alcohol.

- Keep a smile on your face; there will be many photographs taken of both of you.

- Expect things to go wrong on your wedding day. Most likely something will go wrong, and no one will notice it but yourself. Relax and don't let it bother you.

- Preserve the top tier of your wedding cake for your first year anniversary.

- Send a special gift to both sets of parents, such as a small album containing the best photographs of the wedding. Personalize this gift by having it engraved with your names and the date of your wedding.

DON'TS

- Don't get involved in other activities; you will be very busy planning your wedding.

- Don't make any major decisions without discussing it openly with your fiancé.

- Don't be controlling. Be open to other people's ideas.

- Don't overspend your budget; this can be extremely stressful.

- Don't wait until the last minute to hire your service providers. The good ones get booked months in advance.

- Don't try to make everyone happy; it is impossible and will only make your wedding planning more difficult.

- Don't try to impress your friends.

- Don't invite old boyfriends or girlfriends to your wedding, unless both you and your fiancé are friendly with them; you don't want to make anybody uncomfortable.

- Don't try to do "everything." Delegate responsibilities to your fiancé, your parents, and to members of your wedding party.

- Don't rely on friends or family to photograph or videotape your wedding. Hire professionals!

- Don't assume that members of your wedding party know what to do. Give them direction with your Wedding Party Timeline and the *Wedding Party Responsibility Cards,* available at most major bookstores.

- Don't assume your service providers know what to do. Give each of them a copy of your detailed Service Provider Timeline.

- Don't schedule your bachelor party the night before the wedding. You don't want to have a hangover on your special day!

- Don't arrive late at the ceremony!

- Don't drink too much during the reception; you don't want to make a fool of yourself on your most special day!

DO'S & DON'TS

DON'TS (CONT'S)

- Don't flirt with members of the opposite sex.

- Don't allow your guests to drive drunk after the reception; you may be held responsible.

- Don't rub cake in the face of your spouse during the cake-cutting ceremony; your spouse might not appreciate it!

- Don't overeat; this may upset your stomach or make you sleepy.

- Don't leave your reception without saying good-bye to your family and friends.

- Don't drive if you have had too much to drink!

WEDDING PARTY RESPONSIBILITIES

EACH MEMBER OF YOUR WEDDING PARTY has his/her own individual duties and responsibilities. The following is a list of the most important duties for each member of your wedding party.

The most convenient method for conveying this information to members of your wedding party is by purchasing a set of the *Wedding Party Responsibility Cards*, published by Wedding Solutions Publishing. This handy book is available for purchase at all major bookstores.

These cards are attractive and contain all the information your wedding party needs to know to assure a smooth wedding: what to do, how to do it, when to do it, when to arrive, and much more. They also include financial responsibilities as well as the processional, recessional, and altar line-up.

WEDDING PARTY RESPONSIBILITIES

MAID OF HONOR

- Helps bride select attire and address invitations
- Plans bridal shower
- Arrives at dressing site two hours before ceremony to assist bride in dressing
- Arrives dressed at ceremony site one hour before the wedding for photographs
- Arranges the bride's veil and train before the processional and recessional
- Holds bride's bouquet and groom's ring, if no ring bearer, during the ceremony
- Witnesses the signing of the marriage license
- Keeps bride on schedule
- Dances with best man during the bridal party dance
- Helps bride change into her going away clothes
- Mails wedding announcements after the wedding
- Returns bridal slip, if rented

BEST MAN

- Responsible for organizing ushers' activities
- Organizes bachelor party for groom
- Drives groom to ceremony site and sees that he is properly dressed before the wedding
- Arrives dressed at ceremony site one hour before the wedding for photographs
- Brings marriage license to wedding
- Pays the clergyman, musicians, photographer, and any other service providers the day of the wedding
- Holds the bride's ring for the groom, if no ring bearer, until needed by officiant
- Witnesses the signing of the marriage license
- Drives newlyweds to reception, if no hired driver
- Offers first toast at reception, usually before dinner
- Keeps groom on schedule
- Dances with maid of honor during the bridal party dance
- May drive couple to airport or honeymoon suite
- Oversees return of tuxedo rentals for groom and ushers, on time and in good condition

WEDDING PARTY RESPONSIBILITIES

BRIDESMAIDS

- Assist maid/matron of honor in planning bridal shower
- Assist bride with errands and addressing invitations
- Participate in all pre-wedding parties
- Arrive at dressing site two hours before ceremony
- Arrive dressed at ceremony site one hour before the wedding for photographs
- Walk behind ushers in order of height during the processional, either in pairs or in single file
- Sit next to ushers at the head table
- Dance with ushers and other important guests
- Encourage single women to participate in the bouquet-tossing ceremony

USHERS

- Help best man with bachelor party
- Arrive dressed at ceremony site one hour before the wedding for photographs
- Distribute wedding programs and maps to the reception as guests arrive
- Seat guests at the ceremony as follows:

  - If female, offer the right arm
  - If male, walk along his left side
  - If couple, offer right arm to female; male follows a step or two behind
  - Seat bride's guests in left pews
  - Seat groom's guests in right pews
  - Maintain equal number of guests in left and right pews, if possible
  - If a group of guests arrive at the same time, seat the eldest woman first
  - Just prior to the processional, escort groom's mother to her seat; then escort bride's mother to her seat

- Two ushers may roll carpet down the aisle after both mothers are seated
- If pew ribbons are used, two ushers may loosen them one row at a time after the ceremony
- Direct guests to the reception sit
- Dance with bridesmaids and other important guests

WEDDING PARTY RESPONSIBILITIES

BRIDE'S MOTHER

- Helps prepare guest list for bride and her family
- Helps plan the wedding ceremony and reception
- Helps bride select her bridal gown
- Helps bride keep track of gifts received
- Selects her own attire according to the formality and color of the wedding
- Makes accommodations for bride's out of town guests
- Arrives dressed at ceremony site one hour before the wedding for photographs
- Is the last person to be seated right before the processional begins
- Sits in the left front pew to the left of bride's father during the ceremony
- May stand up to signal the start of the processional
- Can witness the signing of the marriage license
- Dances with the groom after the first dance
- Acts as hostess at the reception

BRIDE'S FATHER

- Helps prepare guest list for bride and her family
- Selects attire that complements groom's attire
- Rides to the ceremony with bride in limousine
- Arrives dressed at ceremony site one hour before the wedding for photographs
- After giving bride away, sits in the left front pew to the right of bride's mother
  If divorced, sits in second or third row unless financing the wedding
- When officiant asks, "Who gives this bride away?" answers, "Her mother and I do," or something similar
- Can witness the signing of the marriage license
- Dances with bride after first dance
- Acts as host at the reception

GROOM'S MOTHER

- Helps prepare guest list for groom and his family
- Selects attire that complements mother of the bride's attire
- Makes accommodations for groom's out-of-town guests
- With groom's father, plans rehearsal dinner

- Arrives dressed at ceremony site one hour before the wedding for photographs
- May stand up to signal the start of the processional
- Can witness the signing of the marriage license

GROOM'S FATHER

- Helps prepare guest list for groom and his family
- Selects attire that complements groom's attire
- With groom's mother, plans rehearsal dinner
- Offers toast to bride at rehearsal dinner
- Arrives dressed at ceremony site one hour before the wedding for photographs
- Can witness the signing of the marriage license

FLOWER GIRL

- Usually between the ages of four and eight
- Attends rehearsal to practice, but is not required to attend pre-wedding parties
- Arrives dressed at ceremony site 45 minutes before the wedding for photos
- Carries a basket filled with loose rose petals to strew along bride's path during processional, if allowed by ceremony site
- If very young, may sit with her parents during ceremony

RING BEARER

- Usually between the ages of four and eight
- Attends rehearsal to practice, but is not required to attend pre-wedding parties
- Arrives at ceremony site 45 minutes before the wedding for photograph
- Carries a white pillow with rings attached
- If younger than seven years, carries mock rings
- If very young, may sit with his parents during ceremony
- If mock rings are used, turns the ring pillow over at the end of the ceremony

WEDDING PARTY FORM

Make a copy of this form and give it to your wedding consultant.

PARENTS

	Name	Phone Number	Responsibilities
Bride's Mother:			
Bride's Father:			
Groom's Mother:			
Groom's Father:			

BRIDE'S ATTENDANTS

	Name	Phone Number	Responsibilities
Maid of Honor:			
Matron of Honor:			
Bridesmaid:			
Bridesmaid:			
Bridesmaid:			
Bridesmaid:			
Bridesmaid:			
Bridesmaid:			
Flower Girl:			
Other:			

GROOM'S ATTENDANTS

	Name	Phone Number	Responsibilities
Best Man:			
Usher:			
Usher:			
Usher:			
Usher:			
Usher:			
Usher:			
Ring Bearer:			
Other:			

WHO PAYS
FOR WHAT

BRIDE AND/OR BRIDE'S FAMILY

- Engagement party
- Wedding consultant's fee
- Bridal gown, veil, and accessories
- Wedding stationery, calligraphy, and postage
- Wedding gift for bridal couple
- Groom's wedding ring
- Gifts for bridesmaids
- Bridesmaids' bouquets
- Pre-wedding parties and bridesmaids' luncheon
- Photography and videography
- Bride's medical exam and blood test
- Wedding guest book and other accessories
- Total cost of the ceremony, including location, flowers, music, rental items, and accessories
- Total cost of the reception, including location, flowers, music, rental items, accessories, food, beverages, cake, decorations, favors, etc.
- Transportation for bridal party to ceremony and reception
- Own attire and travel expenses

GROOM AND/OR GROOM'S FAMILY

- Own travel expenses and attire
- Rehearsal dinner
- Wedding gift for bridal couple
- Bride's wedding ring
- Gifts for groom's attendants
- Medical exam for groom including blood test
- Bride's bouquet and going away corsage
- Mothers' and grandmothers' corsages
- All boutonnieres
- Officiant's fee
- Marriage license
- Honeymoon expenses

ATTENDANTS

- Own attire except flowers
- Travel expenses
- Bridal shower paid for by maid of honor and bridesmaids
- Bachelor party paid for by best man and ushers

WEDDING FORMATIONS

THE FOLLOWING SECTION ILLUSTRATES THE TYPICAL CEREMONY formations (processional, recessional, and altar line up) for both Christian and Jewish weddings, as well as the typical formations for the receiving line, head table, and parents' tables at the reception.

These ceremony formations are included in the *Wedding Party Responsibility Cards*, published by Wedding Solutions Publishing, Inc. This attractive set of cards makes it very easy for members of your wedding party to remember their place in these formations.

Give one card to each member of your wedding party... they will appreciate it. This book of cards is available at major bookstores.

*A*LTAR *L*INE *U*P

Bride's Pews

Groom's Pews

ABBREVIATIONS

B=Bride

GF=Groom's Father

G=Groom

GM=Groom's Mother

BM=Best Man

BMa=Bridesmaids

MH=Maid of Honor

U=Ushers

BF=Bride's Father

FG=Flower Girl

BMo=Bride's Mother

RB=Ring Bearer

O=Officiant

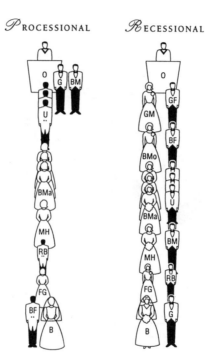

$\mathscr{P}$ROCESSIONAL $\qquad$ $\mathscr{R}$ECESSIONAL

ABBREVIATIONS

B=Bride	GF=Groom's Father	G=Groom	GM=Groom's Mother
BM=Best Man	BMa=Bridesmaids	MH=Maid of Honor	U=Ushers
BF=Bride's Father	FG=Flower Girl	BMo=Bride's Mother	RB=Ring Bearer
O=Officiant			

$\mathcal{A}$LTAR $\mathcal{L}$INE $\mathcal{U}$P

Groom's Pews   Bride's Pews

ABBREVIATIONS

B=Bride   GF=Groom's Father   G=Groom   GM=Groom's Mother
BM=Best Man   BMa=Bridesmaids   MH=Maid of Honor   U=Ushers
BF=Bride's Father   FG=Flower Girl   BMo=Bride's Mother   RB=Ring Bearer
R=Rabbi

JEWISH FORMATIONS

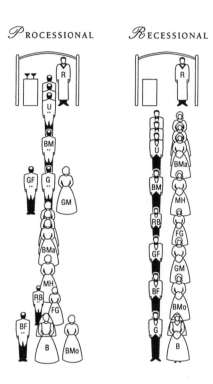

$\mathscr{P}$ROCESSIONAL $\mathscr{R}$ECESSIONAL

ABBREVIATIONS

B=Bride	GF=Groom's Father	G=Groom	GM=Groom's Mother
BM=Best Man	BMa=Bridesmaids	MH=Maid of Honor	U=Ushers
BF=Bride's Father	FG=Flower Girl	BMo=Bride's Mother	RB=Ring Bearer
R=Rabbi			

$\mathscr{R}$ECEIVING $\mathscr{L}$INE

$\mathscr{H}$EAD $\mathscr{T}$ABLE

$\mathscr{P}$ARENTS' $\mathscr{T}$ABLE

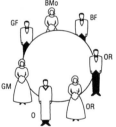

ABBREVIATIONS

B=Bride	GF=Groom's Father	G=Groom	GM=Groom's Mother
BM=Best Man	BMa=Bridesmaids	MH=Maid of Honor	U=Ushers
BF=Bride's Father	OR=Other Relatives	BMo=Bride's Mother	O=Officiant

THINGS TO BRING

TO THE REHEARSAL

BRIDE'S LIST
- ❏ Wedding announcements (maid of honor to mail after wedding)
- ❏ Bridesmaids' gifts (if not already given)
- ❏ Camera and film
- ❏ Fake bouquet or ribbon bouquet from bridal shower
- ❏ Groom's gift (if not already given)
- ❏ Reception maps and wedding programs
- ❏ Rehearsal information and ceremony formations
- ❏ Flower girl basket and ring bearer pillow
- ❏ Seating diagrams for head table and parents' tables
- ❏ Wedding schedule of events/timeline
- ❏ Tape/CD player with wedding music

GROOM'S LIST
- ❏ Bride's gift (if not already given)
- ❏ Marriage license
- ❏ Ushers' gifts (if not already given)
- ❏ Service providers' fees to give to best man or wedding consultant so s/he can pay them at the wedding

THINGS TO BRING

TO THE CEREMONY

BRIDE'S LIST

- Aspirin/Alka Seltzer
- Bobby pins
- Breath spray/mints
- Bridal gown
- Bridal gown box
- Cake knife
- Going away clothes
- Clear nail polish
- Deodorant
- Garter
- Gloves
- Groom's ring
- Guest book
- Hairbrush
- Hair spray
- Headpiece
- Iron
- Jewelry
- Kleenex
- Lint brush
- Luggage
- Make-up
- Mirror
- Nail polish
- Panty hose
- Passport
- Perfume
- Personal camera
- Plume pen for guest book
- Powder
- Purse
- Safety pins
- Scotch tape/masking tape
- Sewing kit
- Shoes
- Something old
- Something new
- Something borrowed
- Something blue
- Sixpence for shoe
- Spot remover
- Straight pins
- Tampons/sanitary napkins
- Toasting goblets
- Toothbrush and paste

GROOM'S LIST

- Airline tickets
- Announcements
- Aspirin/Alka Seltzer
- Breath spray/mints
- Bride's ring
- Going away clothes
- Cologne
- Cuff Links
- Cummerbund
- Deodorant
- Haircomb
- Hair spray
- Kleenex
- Lint brush
- Luggage
- Neck tie
- Passport
- Shirt
- Shoes
- Socks
- Toothbrush and paste
- Tuxedo
- Underwear

WEDDING PLANNING
CALENDAR

THE NEXT SEVERAL MONTHS WILL BE FILLED WITH IMPORTANT DATES. Make sure you allow yourself adequate time to book your ceremony and reception site in advance, schedule meetings with caterers, photographers, florists, bakeries, and still have time to take care of any other wedding planning details.

Use the calendar on the following pages to document your wedding date, parties, all of your appointments, scheduled payments, and any other items you want to complete by a certain date.

If you are planning on a health, fitness, and/or beauty regime during your wedding planning process, write down your routine on this calendar to keep you on track and help you reach your goal.

How to use the calendar: Assign the last calendar page provided for the month your wedding will take place. Then work backwards and simply fill in the month, year, and number of months before your wedding at the top of each page. Then fill in the dates based on each month.

WEDDING PLANNING CALENDAR

Month_____ 20_____ Number of months before wedding _____

Sunday	Monday	Tuesday	Wednesday	Thursday	Friday	Saturday

Notes:_____

WEDDING PLANNING CALENDAR

Month_____ 20_____ Number of months before wedding _____

Sunday	Monday	Tuesday	Wednesday	Thursday	Friday	Saturday

Notes:_____

WEDDING PLANNING CALENDAR

Month_____ 20_____ Number of months before wedding _____

Sunday	Monday	Tuesday	Wednesday	Thursday	Friday	Saturday

Notes:_____

_____

WEDDING PLANNING CALENDAR

Month_____ 20_____ Number of months before wedding _____

Sunday	Monday	Tuesday	Wednesday	Thursday	Friday	Saturday

Notes:_____

WEDDING PLANNING CALENDAR

Month_____ 20_____ Number of months before wedding _____

Sunday	Monday	Tuesday	Wednesday	Thursday	Friday	Saturday

Notes:_____

WEDDING PLANNING CALENDAR

Month_____ 20_____ Number of months before wedding _____

Sunday	Monday	Tuesday	Wednesday	Thursday	Friday	Saturday

Notes:_____

WEDDING PLANNING CALENDAR

Month_____ 20_____ Number of months before wedding _____

Sunday	Monday	Tuesday	Wednesday	Thursday	Friday	Saturday

Notes:_____

Month_____ 20_____ Number of months before wedding _____

Sunday	Monday	Tuesday	Wednesday	Thursday	Friday	Saturday

Notes:_____

WEDDING PLANNING CALENDAR

Month_____ 20_____ Number of months before wedding _____

Sunday	Monday	Tuesday	Wednesday	Thursday	Friday	Saturday

Notes:_____

WEDDING PLANNING CALENDAR

Month_____ 20_____ Number of months before wedding _____

Sunday	Monday	Tuesday	Wednesday	Thursday	Friday	Saturday

Notes:_____

WEDDING PLANNING CALENDAR

Month_____ 20_____ Number of months before wedding _____

Sunday	Monday	Tuesday	Wednesday	Thursday	Friday	Saturday

Notes:_____

WEDDING PLANNING CALENDAR

Month_____ 20_____ Number of months before wedding _____

Sunday	Monday	Tuesday	Wednesday	Thursday	Friday	Saturday

Notes:_____

DATES TO REMEMBER

TELL US ABOUT YOUR WEDDING

We would greatly appreciate you writing to us after your honeymoon to let us know how your wedding went and how much the *Planning the Most Memorable Wedding on Any Budget* helped you in planning your event. We will use this information to continue improving this extensive wedding planner, and we may even use your story in our upcoming book about wedding experiences if you permit us to. We might even ask you to participate in some of our future radio and TV tours where you can tell your own story to the public! Feel free to use additional sheets if necessary.

Dear Elizabeth & Alex:

I want to tell you that the *Planning the Most Memorable Wedding on Any Budget*: (helped a lot), (helped a little), in planning my wedding.

I especially liked your section on:_____. My wedding was on:_____: and it was: (a complete success), (a wild party), (a boring event), (a complete disaster), (the most stressful day of my life).

My comments about your book are:_____
_____
_____
_____

I wish your book had given me information about:_____
_____
_____
_____

The best thing about my wedding was:_____
_____
_____
_____

The worst thing about my wedding was:_____
_____
_____
_____

TELL US ABOUT YOUR WEDDING

The funniest thing about my wedding was:
_____
_____
_____

What made my wedding special or unique was:
_____
_____
_____

My wedding would have been much better if:
_____
_____
_____

This is to authorize Wedding Solutions Publishing, Inc. to use our story in any of their upcoming books. Wedding Solutions Publishing, Inc. (can), (cannot) use our name when telling our story. I also (am), (am not) interested in participating in a radio/TV interview tour.

Bride's Name: _____
Bride's Signature: _____
Groom's Name: _____
Groom's Signature: _____
Address: _____
Home Number: _____ Work Number: _____
E-mail: _____

Mail to Wedding Solutions Publishing, Inc.

Wedding Solutions Publishing, Inc.
7290 Navajo Road, Suite 207
San Diego, California 92119

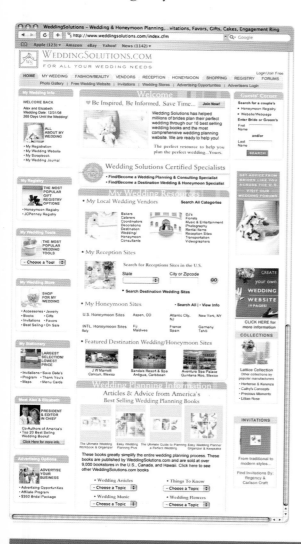

Featuring The Marriott Honeymoon Gift Registry

With The Marriott Honeymoon Gift Registry, Every Gift is an Experience

Marriott, in partnership with WeddingSolutions.com, is now offering a Honeymoon Gift Registry that will allow your guests to contribute to the honeymoon of your dreams. You will receive a Marriott GiftCard in a beautiful keepsake album, loaded with your guests' contributions such as room nights, romantic dinners, relaxing massages, and much more. Create an unforgettable honeymoon at any of the thousands of beautiful Marriott hotels and resorts worldwide. No service fees or hidden charges for you or your guests!

Log on to WeddingSolutions.com/MarriottRegistry for details

Co-Authors of Over 30 Best-Selling Wedding Planning Books and Founders of WeddingSolutions.com

Wedding Solutions Publishing, Inc.

Alex and Elizabeth Lluch are the President and Editor in Chief, respectively, of Wedding Solutions Publishing, Inc., the largest and most celebrated wedding consulting and publishing company in America.

This husband and wife team has been in the wedding industry for over 15 years. Their books have helped millions of couples plan the wedding of their dreams.

Alex and Elizabeth are famous for describing the wedding planning process in a very simple and effective way. This has made their books the most sought-after wedding planners in North America. Their books are sold at over six thousand stores in the U.S., Canada, and Hawaii. Their books are also used by national companies such as JCPenney, Kay Jewelers, Jared Jewelers, and many more as incentive gift items.

At the present time, Alex and Elizabeth sell over 500,000 wedding books a year. This means that about one-third of all brides who plan a traditional wedding use Alex and Elizabeth's wedding books to plan their weddings.

WeddingSolutions.com

Alex and Elizabeth Lluch are also the President and Editor in Chief, respectively, of WeddingSolutions.com, the most comprehensive and easy-to-use wedding planning website in the world. WeddingSolutions.com helps couples plan their wedding from start to finish. WeddingSolutions.com has the highest ranking on all major search engines including Google, Yahoo, and MSN. WeddingSolutions.com is proud to be the exclusive wedding content provider for 39 NBC affiliate television websites.

Certification Programs

Alex and Elizabeth Lluch are also proud to be the authors and publishers of the most extensive certification programs in the bridal market. The Wedding Planning and Consulting Certification program is for anyone interested in helping others plan the wedding of their dreams, or in starting a business as a wedding consultant. The Destination Wedding and Honeymoon Certification program is designed for travel agents who wish to become specialists in this growing field. This program has received the highest review by the Travel Institute of North America and counts as 10 credits for continuing education.

Below are a few of Alex and Elizabeth's best-selling wedding planning books

The Complete Wedding
Planner & Organizer

Making Your Wedding
Beautiful, Memorable,
& Unique

Planning the Most
Memorable Wedding
On Any Budget

The Ultimate Wedding
Workbook & Organizer

The Ultimate Wedding
Planner & Organizer

Easy Wedding Planner
Organizer & Keepsake

Easy Wedding
Planning Plus

The Ultimate Wedding
Workbook & Organizer

The Ultimate Guide to the
World's Best Wedding &
Honeymoon Destinations

The Very Best Wedding
Planner & Organizer

The Very Best Wedding
Planning Guide

The Ultimate Guide
to Planning the
Perfect Wedding

The Ultimate Wedding
Planning Guide

The Ultimate
Groom's Guide

The Ultimate Guide
to Wedding Music

Wedding Party
Responsibility Cards

Easy Wedding
Planning

The Ultimate Wedding
Name & Address
Change Kit

Easy Wedding
Shopping Guide

The Ultimate Wedding
Planning Calendar